the Cook Book

For Ella and Paddy who inspire us every day.
And for all of their generation — may good
food bring joy throughout your lives.

Paul + Alison Lindley

First published in Great Britain in 2013 by
Hamlyn, a division of Octopus Publishing Group Ltd
Endeavour House
189 Shaftesbury Avenue
London
WC2H 8JY
www.octopusbooks.co.uk

An Hachette UK Company
www.hachette.co.uk

Disclaimer

A few recipes include nuts and nut derivatives. Anyone
with a known nut allergy must avoid these. Children
under the age of 3 with a family history of nut allergy,
asthma, eczema or any type of allergy are also advised to
avoid eating dishes that contain nuts.

Some recipes contain honey. It is advised not to feed
honey to children under 12 months old.

Every care should be taken when cooking with and for
children. Neither the author, the contributors nor the
publisher can accept any liability for any consequences
arising from the use of this book, or the
information contained herein.

Ella's Kitchen (Brands) Limited asserts the moral right to be
identified as the author of this work.
ISBN 9780600626411

A CIP catalogue record for this book is available from the
British Library

Typeset in Cooper Light and Ella's Kitchen
Printed and bound in China

Created by Ella's Kitchen and Harris + Wilson

10 9 8 7 6 5 4 3

Design and styling: Anita Mangan
Photographer: Jonathan Cherry
Managing editor: Judy Barratt
Design assistant: Abigail Read
Assistant production manager: Lucy Carter
Food stylist: Vicki Savage
Recipe testing: Emma Jane Frost

Publisher's notes

Standard level spoon measures are used
in the recipes:
1 tablespoon = one 15 ml spoon
1 teaspoon = one 5 ml spoon

Both metric and imperial measurements are
given for the recipes. Use one set of measures
only, not a mixture of both.

Ovens should be preheated to the specified temperature.
If using a fan-assisted oven, follow the manufacturer's
instructions for adjusting the time and temperature.

Medium eggs have been used throughout, unless otherwise
specified. Herbs are fresh, unless otherwise specified. Use
low-salt stock, and avoid adding salt to recipes altogether.

Freezing advice

Freeze food in a freezer set at -18°C (0°F). Meat
dishes freeze safely for up to 4 weeks; vegetarian
dishes (including fruit pies), cakes and biscuits
can freeze for up to 3 months. Always label your
foods with the date of freezing. When defrosting,
always do so covered in the fridge, or in an
airtight container submersed in cold water, or
in a microwave. Eat, cook or reheat foods (as
appropriate) as soon as they are defrosted. When
reheating, always do so until piping hot all the way
through. Do not refreeze.

the Cook Book

100 yummy recipes to inspire big and little cooks

hamlyn

Contents

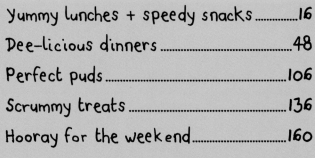

Foreword by Ella's dad

My wife Alison and I became first-time parents when our daughter Ella was born. The new responsibility, the sense of fulfilment and the unlimited outpouring of love are – I'm sure – felt by virtually every new parent. Parenthood really is life-changing. By the time our son Paddy was born, I'd been an active father for three years – and I loved it.

I experienced first-hand the challenges of weaning and the issues involved with introducing two babies (and then toddlers) to new foods. Ella, like the vast majority of little ones, was selective about what she wanted to try, often with no consistency from one day to the next. My solution was to do what I do best: to be silly and childlike. I thought up food-based games. I tried to encourage her to look at her food, and to touch it, smell it and even listen to it, before finally eating it. I invented stories and made up songs; I created imaginary friends and performed 'magic'. I turned mealtimes into events that were messy, noisy and interactive. Ella laughed and I laughed. Best of all, Ella showed willingness to experiment with and enjoy her food. My efforts worked with Paddy, too.

Then, I had my 'lightbulb' moment: healthy food could be – and should be – fun for young kids. This single notion was to be the inspiration for Ella's Kitchen. I gave up my job and set about creating a range of foods for babies, toddlers and young children. I wanted to develop a brand that would bring together three elements that often work against each other in prepared children's food: healthiness, handiness and fun.

At Ella's we always try to look at life from a child's point of view – with an open mind and with all our senses. My strong belief is that the more a young child is involved with his or her food – whether that's choosing it, preparing it, playing with it or eating it independently – the more likely he or she is to give it a try and to go on to enjoy it. With such a positive start, children are far more likely to grow up to have a healthy attitude not just towards mealtimes, but towards their whole diet and overall wellbeing, too.

We've created this book to build further on the Ella's Kitchen ethos – to help even the youngest of children develop healthy eating habits that will last their lifetime. I hope that it will give you and your family far more than recipes for fantastic children's food. I hope that the shared experience of creating dishes together – from making the shopping list and buying and preparing the ingredients to discovering how they feel and spotting their rainbow of colours – will help to strengthen your bond. The ultimate expression of this bond is when you sit down to eat together with big smiles, enjoying the meal that you have created.

Our Ella's Kitchen family has had great fun experimenting as we've developed the ideas for this book. Now that it has found its way to your family kitchen, I hope that your mealtime experiences are equally as good!

Keep smiling

Paul

Paul, Ella's dad x
Follow me on Twitter: @Paul_Lindley

In Ella's own words

Ever since I was very young, I've loved playing and experimenting with food. Some of my favourite memories are centred around foody things. One of my earliest recollections of cooking is from when I was about four and my friends and I created a chocolate café, complete with chocolate cookies, chocolate soup and chocolate milkshake – although I'm pretty sure everything tasted the same!

My favourite school subject is Food Technology – we learn how to cook more independently and how to make more complex dishes. I love coming home from school on Mondays with a freshly made pizza or pasta bake.

All of my family enjoy creating new meals and our oven is never put to rest. One of my favourite sensations is when I wake up on a Sunday morning to the mouth-watering smell of pancakes, or when I get home from school to the appetising aroma of dinner. Whether it's curry or roast, my dad always makes sure that our meals are healthy and yummy at the same time. My brother and I are both very involved with the family's cooking and we often take it in turns to make dinner.

Once, for my grandma's birthday, we each cooked a course. My little brother cooked the appetiser; my dad, a starter; my mum, the main; and I made dessert. It made my grandma's birthday extra amazingly, superbly special! I think that letting kids get involved with food from a young age and letting them try new, exciting things is very important. I hope you have loads of fun with our cook book!

Ella x

Ella, now aged 13

Our cook book

A bit about using this book

We hope that this book is far more than just a cook book. It's about encouraging your children to embark upon a lifetime's adventure with food. As you involve them in every step of the cooking process, you'll help them to develop food confidence. Their curiosity will turn them into excited culinary explorers – they'll want to smell, touch and taste the ingredients and they'll love how foods transform during cooking. By taking time to follow a recipe together, you are sharing quality time during which you laugh together, enjoy each other's company *and* make something yummy.

From the beginning

If you're a first-time parent embarking upon weaning, take a look at our simple weaning guide on pages 10–11. Our tips provide the essence of how to introduce an exciting array of foods to your baby from their first mouthfuls. If you have a toddler and a baby and want to make meals that will accommodate both, look out for the easy to 'mash down' icon (see opposite), which flags up the recipes that are also great to mash for your tiny family members.

Getting stuck in

Tots and toddlers make wonderful helpers, and at Ella's we believe that messiness is all part of the fun: there's lots to stir, mix, squish, pour, squeeze and decorate. We love it when little fingers are prepared to feel the textures of different foods during the cooking process and then make foods look beautiful on the plate – even if that's just arranging fruit slices in a pattern.

Lots of the recipes have suggestions for how little ones can help; not to mention our inspirational activity pages, which are intended to create general excitement about the world of food.

At the end of the book there are some handy stickers. You can use them as rewards for your children for super helping or fabulous eating and as markers for their favourite recipes, too.

Saving time

We know you're busy and it's been really important to us that we provide you with recipes that are suitable for your lifestyle. As a result, the dishes are not only nutritious and delicious, they're easy to make. They've all come from parents like you and have been road-tested by Ella's Kitchen families, and our friends.

Whenever we can we've included handy hints and shortcuts to help save you time. For example, we've suggested when you could use an Ella's Kitchen pouch as a short-cut for a sauce or to add colour. Then, we've included a chapter called 'Hooray for the Weekend', which you can dip into when you have more time to cook as a family.

Sensible shopping lists

All the recipes in the book use healthy ingredients. Our team of nutritionists has selected and approved every one to ensure that you can provide your children with a diet to nourish their growing bodies. We've avoided using sugar and salt whenever the recipe allows, preferring instead to sweeten and season with alternatives, such as honey, maple syrup, herbs and spices. Whenever you can, use low-salt or no-salt versions of stock cubes and other ingredients that might already have salt in them.

We recommend that you use organic foods, especially for the fresh ingredients. We believe that organic farmers produce their foods using the purest farming standards.

We've tried to ensure that the recipes call for ingredients that you can find easily and that your children will be able to identify. All should be available in your local supermarket and you may even already have lots of them in your cupboards.

We believe that to have a truly healthy relationship with food, children should never feel guilty or awkward about anything they eat. Healthy puddings – and treats for special occasions – are fine and all our sweet recipes minimise the use of refined sugar.

Key to icons

At the top of every recipe you'll find a combination of the following icons to help make cooking for, and with, your little ones as easy as it can be.

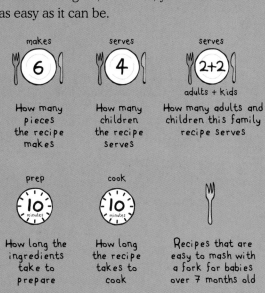

makes

6

How many pieces the recipe makes

serves

4

How many children the recipe serves

serves

2+2

adults + kids

How many adults and children this family recipe serves

prep

10 minutes

How long the ingredients take to prepare

cook

10 minutes

How long the recipe takes to cook

Recipes that are easy to mash with a fork for babies over 7 months old

First foods for tiny taste buds

1 When to wean

All babies are different – some may be ready for solid foods earlier than others; and some will take to weaning more quickly than others. However, recommendations are that you wait until your baby reaches 17 weeks of age before beginning weaning and that the best age to start is at around 6 months.

Look for signs that your baby is ready for weaning. Putting everything in his or her mouth is one good sign, as is being able to sit up without support.

2 Ready, steady, go!

Wakey wakey

When you begin weaning, offer food at times when your baby is alert and happy.

Little by little

At the start, try offering food in the middle of or just after your baby's usual milk feed.

Playing with food

Try giving your little one some blanched veggie chunks to play with while he or she is eating. Exploring shapes, colours, textures and smells helps babies to love new foods.

Baby knows best

Most babies know when they've had enough to eat. If your little one doesn't seem to want any more, don't force the issue.

Smoothly does it

Smooth purées give the best texture for tiny tummies, so whiz up some veggies or fruit with a little of your baby's usual milk. Veggies and hard fruits (such as apples) will need to be peeled, chopped, then steamed or boiled until soft before you blend them; soft fruits (such as bananas) can be blended straightaway.

3 Taste explosion

Babies have 30,000 taste buds in their tiny mouths – that's 3 times more than grown-ups – so new food is big news.

One by one

It's best to give babies individual foods at first so that they can grow accustomed to the different flavours, colours and textures. To really make tiny taste buds zing, start with more unusual flavours such as broccoli and cauliflower, and some less sweet fruits, including green apples and pears. Keep introducing colours and flavours until you're cooking up a rainbow of foods.

Week 1: once a day

Build up from 1 spoonful of purée to about 5 spoonfuls per meal by the end of week 1. Try some of these yummy fruit and veg this week:

 Broccoli
 Cauliflower
 Pear

 Spinach
Green beans
Cabbage

Week 2: once or twice a day

Your baby can slurp up about 5 spoonfuls of purée at each meal. Try some of these yummy fruit and veg this week:

 Apple
 Green beans
 Potato

 Spinach
 Carrot
 Parsnip

Week 3: Twice a day

Offer up to 10 spoonfuls at each meal – a feast! Try some of these yummy fruit and veg this week:

Sweet potato
Banana
Broccoli
Cabbage
Pear
Blueberries
Apple

Week 4: 2 or 3 times a day

10 or more spoonfuls will tingle tiny taste buds at breakfast, lunch and dinner – let your baby tell you when he or she has had enough. Try some of these yummy fruit and veg this week:

 Carrot
 Broccoli
 Pear
 Banana

 Cauliflower
 Mango
 Apple

Mixing it up

Once your little one has got used to lots of individual flavours, it's time to make things even more interesting and mix up the tastes in exciting combinations. Here are 5 yummy flavour combos guaranteed to get tiny taste buds going.

Mango + strawberry + baby rice
Papaya + sweet potato + pear
Carrot + pea + apple
Blackberry + apple + pear
Mango + apple + lime

From mush to mash + beyond

All babies are different and they may reach the following stages a bit earlier or later than we've suggested here, but that's totally normal. Remember that lots of the recipes in this book can be mashed up or blended for babies at Stage 2 onwards, too.

Look for the 'mash down' icon

4–6 months

How do I eat?
I can move food from side to side in my mouth, using my tongue.

What can I eat?
Smooth purée with no bits, such as baby porridge and whizzed-up softly cooked fruit and vegetables.

7–9 months

How do I eat?
I can mush up soft lumps with my tongue and I can grasp finger foods in my hand and put them in my mouth. Let me hold a spoon and I'll have a go at scooping.

What can I eat?
Fork-mashed fruit and veg; soft-cooked minced beef and turkey, and mashed-down lentils and beans. I love soft finger foods, such as slices of melon, peach and banana, or soft-cooked carrot sticks.

10–12 months

How do I eat?
I can chew! I may have a tooth or two, so I love to munch on larger chunks. Finger foods with a bit of bite will help to soothe my teething gums.

What can I eat?
Whole peas, beans and sweetcorn, firmer cooked veg and minced meat, as well as baby biscuits and raw vegetable sticks.

Now I am One

How do I eat?
I'm great at munching lots of new foods with my toothy pegs. I can pick up smaller pieces of food with my pincer grip.

What can I eat?
Softly cooked small chunks of meat; stir-fries with veggie strips; raisins, blueberries and other whole berries.

Tiny tums and energy needs

Babies need lots of calories and nutrients to fuel their super-fast growth. In fact, per kilo of their body weight, they need more calories than you do!

However, your baby's tummy is still tiny and it can't hold a lot of food in one go. From around 7 months, it's important to give him or her 3 meals and 2 or 3 nutritious snacks each day, as well as at least 500 ml/17 fl oz of his or her usual milk.

I use up loads of energy because I'm growing fast and learning to roll, crawl, pull myself up and even take my first tiny steps.

Handy healthy snacks

Try your baby on the following healthy snacks from around 7–9 months old, depending upon when your baby is ready.

- ☺ Pitta slices with hummus or cream cheese
- ☺ Breadsticks and dips
- ☺ Cubes of cheese
- ☺ Blueberries, raspberries and sliced grapes
- ☺ Cooked broccoli 'trees' and carrot sticks
- ☺ Cooked pasta shapes – try the spinach and tomato varieties to provide some interesting colours

Fruity banana bars

Try these healthy snack bars from 10–12 months old – they are great for little ones on the go.

1. Mash ½ banana and mix it with 3–4 tablespoons fine milled oats.
2. Stir in 2 tablespoons raisins.
3. Form the mixture into small bars, adding more oats if you need to make the dough firmer.
4. Place the bars on a lightly greased baking sheet and cook at 180°C/350°F/Gas Mark 4 for 10–15 minutes until firm.
5. Allow to cool and enjoy.

Learning about food

Our research shows that children develop healthier eating habits if they can explore food not just with their mouths and taste buds, but with all their amazing senses. Then, as they get older, you can teach them in the simplest terms how all that delicious goodness is helping them to grow up strong and healthy.

Good in every sense

Even the tiniest tots can learn to appreciate the sights, smells and textures of their food. As your little one learns to express himself or herself using face-pulling, sounds and eventually words, he or she will find many ways to tell you what they think. Even if at the start you're doing all the talking, your baby is taking it all in and will respond with delighted coos, squeals – and grimaces!

Play a game of squeezing eyes tight as you present foods with different smells. Older children will be able to describe or even identify them.

Looks lovely

Lots of different colours and shapes on the plate look more appetising for little ones. Each time your baby reaches for a food, talk about the colour and, when foods are whole, the shapes.

Sounds scrummy

What makes an onion sizzle in a pan? How does a carrot stick crunch? How is that different from the crunch of an apple? What's the sound of a smoothie slurp? When we like something, we say 'Mmmmm'. Encourage your little one to listen to foody sounds as you cook, eat and enjoy their meals together.

Tastes terrific

There's no reason why exploring tastes can't become child's play. By Stage 2 of weaning, you can introduce some really zingy flavours. Sit at the table and play a tasting game. Try little pieces of pineapple, or strips of red, green and yellow pepper – any distinctive flavours work really well. Poke out a tongue and give foods an exploratory lick.

Smells super

Our sense of smell is closely linked to our sense of taste. Encourage your baby to smell his or her food before eating it. Lead the way: waft it under your own nose and make happy, yummy sounds before you offer it to your baby, who will soon learn to take a sniff and copy what you do.

Feels fab

Allow your baby to pick up his or her food to feel how bumpy, rough or smooth it is. Again, you do the describing. Remember that babies do a lot of 'feeling' with their tongues as well as with their fingers.

Eat a rainbow

Exploring different colours in food is not just about creating excitement – eating all the colours of the rainbow will give your baby the whole spectrum of goodness that he or she needs to grow up great.

Here's our rainbow of favourite foods:

Red: Cherry, cranberry, pepper, radish, raspberry, red onion, strawberry, tomato

Orange: Apricot, butternut squash, carrot, mango, orange, papaya, peach, pepper, pumpkin, sweet potato

Yellow: Banana, lemon, parsnip, pineapple, starfruit

Green: Apple, artichoke, asparagus, broccoli, cabbage, courgette, grape, kiwi, lime, pear, spinach

Blue: Blueberry

Purple: Beetroot, blackberry, blackcurrant, plum

Colour a rainbow! Which colours of fruit and veg has your little one eaten this week? Make a picture using those colours.

The wheel of scrummy goodness

It's good to introduce children to the idea that food makes us strong. Use our Wheel of Scrummy Goodness as a starting point to teach your toddler about the nutrients that help keep him or her healthy.

Vitamin A to help you see

Vitamin C for healthy gums

Iron for a healthy brain

B-vitamins for bouncy energy

Calcium for strong bones

Zinc for super-immunity

yummy lunches + speedy snacks

Have fantastically fruity fun with my veeeery streeeetchy cheese on toast.

Love, Ella x

Brilliant butternut squash soup

This soup hits the spot for a family welly walk – these children loved it. Perhaps it's the soup's sweet, rich flavour that got their senses going – or the *reeeally* bright orange. Add the cardamom if your little one is up for trying new flavours.

What you need

About 1.4 kg/3 lb 2 oz **butternut squash**, cut into 2.5 cm/1 in dice

Olive oil, for roasting

8 **sage** leaves, finely chopped

50 g/1¾ oz **unsalted butter**

1 **onion**, chopped

Seeds from 10 **cardamom pods**, crushed (optional)

900 ml/1½ pints **vegetable stock**

Finely grated rind and juice of 1 **orange**

Crème fraîche, to serve

What to do

1. Preheat the oven to 200°C/400°F/Gas Mark 6.

2. Put the squash cubes in a roasting tray, sprinkle with a little olive oil and scatter over the chopped sage. Toss the cubes so that they are well coated in the oil, then roast them in the oven for 15–20 minutes or until the cubes are soft and turning golden. Remove the squash from the oven and set aside.

3. Melt the butter in a large saucepan over a medium heat, then add the onion and fry until soft. Add the crushed cardamom pods (if using), the vegetable stock and the orange rind and juice. Then add the squash. Give it all a stir and bring to a boil. Reduce the heat and simmer for 15–20 minutes, until all the ingredients are soft and pulpy and the liquid has reduced a little. Remove the pan from the heat and use a hand blender to whiz the mixture until smooth.

4. Serve the soup with a dollop of crème fraîche.

Can I help?

Squashy tasks

Digging out the squash seeds with a spoon is a great way to get children involved in the early stages of the soup, as well as sprinkling over the sage before roasting. Ask your little one to watch as you blend the soup – can they see how it changes before their very eyes? Take care that the hot liquid doesn't splash, though.

Cheeky chicken, leek + sweetcorn soup

You need just 5 ingredients for this filling and nourishing soup. It's super-speedy to prepare – our Ella's tester had never made soup before and declared this one to be easy peasy. Your children will love the sweetness of the corn.

What you need

800 ml/1¼ pints **chicken stock**

325 g/11½ oz **canned sweetcorn**

250 g/9 oz **leeks**, finely chopped

225 g/8 oz **cooked chicken breast**, cut into tiny pieces

A small handful of **flat-leaf parsley**, finely chopped, to serve (optional)

What to do

1. Blend 150 ml/¼ pint of the stock with half of the sweetcorn until smooth, then transfer the purée and the rest of the stock to a saucepan and bring it to the boil.

2. Add the leeks to the stock mixture and lower the heat to simmer for 10 minutes until the leeks have softened.

3. Add the cooked chicken pieces and the remaining sweetcorn to the stock mixture. Simmer for a further 4–5 minutes until the chicken and sweetcorn are heated through.

4. Pour the soup into bowls and sprinkle with some freshly chopped parsley to serve (if using).

20

Veggie-tastic samosas

makes **6** · prep **20** minutes · cook **20-25** minutes

Easy for tiny hands to grasp and bursting with good stuff, our veggie samosas are a perfect snack served at home, on the go, or in a lunchbox. Use our handy folding guide to make beautiful little parcels.

What you need

300 g/10½ oz **swede**, finely diced

100 g/3½ oz **carrots**, finely diced

4 tablespoons **frozen peas**, defrosted

1 teaspoon **garam masala**

Lemon juice, to taste

Vegetable oil, for spraying

4 sheets of **filo pastry**

Nigella seeds, for sprinkling

What to do

1. Preheat the oven to 180°C/350°F/Gas Mark 4.

2. In a frying pan, dry-fry the vegetables for 5 minutes over a medium heat until slightly softened. Season with the garam masala, and add a squeeze of lemon juice to taste.

3. Spray two sheets of the filo pastry with oil and then sandwich them together. Cut the sandwiched sheets into 3 strips.

4. Blob a spoonful of the vegetable filling at the bottom corner of each strip of pastry. One by one fold the strips as shown in our folding diagram to create 3 perfectly formed samosas.

5. Repeat steps 3 and 4 for the remaining filo sheets, then spray each samosa with a little more oil and sprinkle with nigella seeds.

6. Place the samosas on a baking sheet and cook in the oven for 15–20 minutes or until lightly browned. Serve warm or cold.

Handy samosa folding guide

Cut the filo pastry into 3 equally sized strips. Put a blob of filling in the bottom corner of each one and fold over and over ...

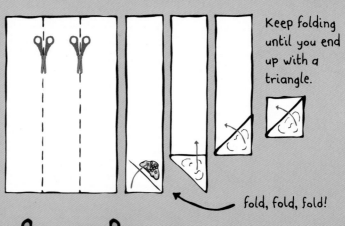

Keep folding until you end up with a triangle.

fold, fold, fold!

Very nice dips for crunchy veg sticks

Fed up with dipping into hummus or mayo? You'll get your little ones happily munching and crunching vegetable sticks all day with these tasty, adventurous dips that are full of complementary flavours and textures. Carrot, celery, cucumber and pepper make the perfect dipping sticks.

Aubergine, pine nut + tomato dip

serves **4** prep **5** minutes cook **45** minutes

1 large **aubergine**

25 g/1 oz **pine nuts**

2 tablespoons **sun-dried tomato purée**

1. Preheat the oven to 200°C/400°F/Gas Mark 6.

2. Prick the aubergine all over with a fork and place it in the oven; bake it for 45 minutes until soft. Allow to cool.

3. In a small frying pan, dry-fry the pine nuts until golden.

4. Scoop the aubergine flesh from the skin and place it in a bowl with the pine nuts and tomato purée. Blend to a coarse paste with a hand blender.

Roast pepper, cream cheese + basil dip

serves **4** prep **5** minutes cook **30** minutes

2 **red peppers**

1 teaspoon **olive oil**

200 g/7 oz **cream cheese**

8 **basil** leaves, finely chopped

1. Preheat the oven to 200°C/400°F/Gas Mark 6.

2. Rub the peppers with the oil and place them on a baking sheet. Roast the peppers for 30 minutes until slightly charred, then place them in a large plastic bag and allow to cool. Peel off the skin and remove the seeds.

3. Place the pepper flesh in a food processor with the cream cheese and blend to a coarse paste. Stir in the basil.

24

Smoked mackerel dip

serves **4** prep **5** minutes

2 **smoked mackerel** fillets, skin and bones removed

5 tablespoons **low-fat natural yogurt**

1. Place the mackerel and yogurt in a food processor and blend to a coarse paste. Or, if you don't have a processor, use a hand blender; or flake the fish into a bowl and mash it with a fork, then stir through the yogurt.

Crunchy veggie dipping sticks

Roast pepper, cream cheese + basil dip

Aubergine, pine nut + tomato dip

Smoked mackerel dip

Bubble + squeak

serves **8** · prep **5** minutes · cook **12** minutes

Somehow even the greenest greens taste great in bubble and squeak and these little veggie fritters are a brilliant way to use up some leftover veg.

What you need

2–3 tablespoons **olive oil**

½ **onion**, finely chopped (or a couple of spring onions)

450 g/1 lb **potatoes**, cooked and mashed

225 g/8 oz cooked **Brussels sprouts**, chopped (or broccoli or cabbage)

½ teaspoon **dried mixed herbs** (or some fresh parsley)

2 **eggs**, beaten

Freshly ground **black pepper**, to taste

What to do

1. Heat 1 tablespoon of the oil in a frying pan and fry the onion over a low heat for 3–4 minutes until soft.

2. Put the mashed potato and sprouts in a bowl and stir. Add the cooked onion, herbs and eggs, season with black pepper, and mix well.

3. Put a further 1 tablespoon of the oil in the frying pan and warm over a medium heat.

4. Fry spoonfuls of the mixture for about 6–8 minutes, turning once using a fish slice, until lightly browned on both sides. (You may need to cook the mixture in batches – using some more oil, if necessary – depending upon the size of your pan.)

5. Serve immediately with a handful of grilled cherry tomatoes and any leftover cold meat you have to hand.

Listen up!

Bubble and squeak is so called because the potato and vegetables make popping and squeaking sounds as they cook in the pan. Ask your little one to listen out for them.

Rainbow stir-fry

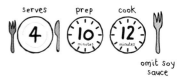

serves 4 · prep 10 minutes · cook 12 minutes

omit soy sauce

Simple, fresh ingredients in this stir-fry create a colourful lunch or supper that everyone can enjoy. You don't have to stick to the vegetables we've given here – introduce new ones every time you cook the dish and see if you can make your way through the rainbow.

What you need

2 tablespoons **sunflower oil**

2 **chicken breasts** (about 300 g/10½ oz), cut into strips

1 **carrot**, cut into thick matchsticks

1 **red pepper**, cut into thick strips

100 g/3½ oz **baby sweetcorn**, halved

1 **courgette**, cut into thick matchsticks

4 **spring onions**, cut into 4 cm/1½ inch lengths

2 tablespoons **sun-dried tomato purée**

1 tablespoon **soy sauce**

What to do

1. Heat 1 tablespoon of the oil in a large frying pan or wok and fry the chicken strips for 4 minutes or until cooked through. Add the carrot, pepper and sweetcorn, cover and leave to fry for 4 minutes.

2. Add the remaining oil, then add the courgette and spring onion and stir-fry for 4 minutes until the green vegetables are warmed through and the sweetcorn and chicken are starting to turn golden.

3. Stir in the tomato purée and soy sauce and cook for 1 minute more. Serve immediately – it's delicious on a mound of brown rice.

Eat a rainbow

Ask little ones to identify the colours of the rainbow in the vegetables you're using. What other vegetables would make up the missing colours?

Colour me in

Quickly does it quiche

serves 2+2 adults + kids | prep 20 minutes | cook 50 minutes

Perfect for a family lunch or a picnic, this easy-peasy quiche is quick to make and great for little hands to hold while munching. You could make it ahead and freeze it in bite-sized portions, which makes it handy for a lunch or snack on the run.

What you need

350 g/12 oz ready-made **shortcrust pastry**

1 tablespoon **sunflower oil**

1 large **onion**, sliced

250 g/9 oz **unsmoked back bacon**, roughly chopped

3 **eggs**, beaten

2 tablespoons finely chopped **parsley** or **thyme**

100 ml/3½ fl oz **whole milk**

50 g/1¾ oz **Cheddar cheese**, grated

Go veggie

For a vegetarian option, fry the onion with 200 g/7 oz carrot and 200 g/7 oz diced aubergine for 5 minutes. Allow to cool, then arrange in the base of the pastry case. Pour over the milk and egg mixture, scatter with the Cheddar, then cook as in the meat version.

What to do

1. Preheat the oven to 200°C/400°F/Gas Mark 6.

2. Roll out the pastry on a floured surface and use it to line a 22 cm/8½ inch round quiche tin. Place a piece of scrunched-up parchment paper inside the pastry casing and fill it with some baking beans (or dried lentils if you can't get hold of baking beans).

3. Place the tin on a baking sheet and bake blind for 10 minutes until the pastry is just starting to colour. Remove the baking beans and parchment and return the pastry to the oven for a further 5 minutes until golden.

4. Meanwhile, heat the oil in a large frying pan and fry the onion and bacon together for 5 minutes until cooked. In a bowl or large measuring jug, mix together the eggs, herbs and milk.

5. Scatter the bacon and onion mixture evenly into the baked pastry case and pour in the milk and egg mixture. Scatter over the Cheddar. Bake in the oven for 25–30 minutes until golden.

choo choo

Clever tomato sauce

serves 4 · prep 15 minutes · cook 12 minutes

This sauce is clever for 2 reasons: first, we can think of lots of ways to use it –
see opposite for 5 of them – and, second, it's packed to the brim with veggie goodness.

What you need

1 **carrot**, diced

200 g/7 oz **butternut squash**, diced

50 g/1¾ oz **frozen peas**, defrosted

415 g/14¾ oz can **baked beans**

400 g/14 oz can **chopped tomatoes**

200 g/7 oz **tomatoes**, chopped

What to do

1. In a saucepan of boiling water, boil the carrot, squash and peas for 7–8 minutes until tender, then drain them and return them to the pan. Keeping the pan off the heat, add the baked beans and purée the mixture with a hand blender until smooth.

2. Return the pan to the heat. Add both the canned and fresh tomatoes and bring everything to the boil. Reduce the heat and simmer for 4–5 minutes until the fresh tomatoes are soft and pulpy. Remove the pan from the heat and purée again until you have a beautifully smooth sauce.

Freeze!

This clever tomato sauce is perfect for freezing in suitable portion sizes – you'll have a healthy and delicious meal at hand for even the busiest days.

Grow your own

Turn your windowsill into a microleaf garden with edible plants that are quick to grow and scrummy to eat. What better way to learn where food comes from?

1

Find your flavours

Rocket, cress, basil and pea shoots all make brilliant microplants – you can harvest their baby leaves within 2 weeks. Choose some greens you'll use – rocket for pizza, basil for pasta sauce, cress for sandwiches. Yum!

② Paint a pot

Little brown pots are the perfect canvas for tiny tot decorations. Find some stickers and some paints and get creative. Spots, stripes or splodges – anything goes.

③ Plant the seeds

Fill the pots with damp soil and scatter in some seeds. Sprinkle over a little more soil and place your pots on a sunny windowsill.

Turn your pot into a face with googly eyes and sticker-lips, then grow some cress in it. Soon enough your face has grown green hair!

Tea-set milk jugs make perfect mini-watering cans for tiny fingers and tiny plants.

④ Harvest the leaves

Remember to talk about the leaves – their colour, shape and smell – as you pick. Use them straightaway.

Fantastically fruity cheese on toast

makes 1 prep 5 minutes cook 4–6 minutes

This is a new dimension in cheese on toast that needs both hands to eat it. Teaming up creamy mozzarella with juicy cranberry sauce is just genius. Serve it as a snack at any time of the day (and you'll probably want to eat one yourself).

What you need

2 thick slices **farmhouse white bread**

Unsalted butter, for spreading

1 tablespoon **cranberry sauce**

1 slice **ham**

50 g/1¾ oz **mozzarella cheese**, sliced

What to do

1. Lightly butter 1 side of each slice of bread. Turn 1 slice unbuttered side up and spread over the cranberry sauce. Top with the ham and slices of mozzarella. Sandwich with the remaining slice of bread, butter side up.

2. Heat a small frying pan and dry-fry the sandwich for 2–3 minutes on each side until the bread is golden and the mozzarella has melted. Serve immediately.

Make it streeeetch!

Have a stringy cheese competition. Everyone takes a bite and the one who can make their cheese stretch the furthest is the winner!

Very veggie couscous

There are no fewer than 7 fruit and veggies in this delicious meal. The tiny couscous grains and soft consistency make this a brilliant lunch for learning to use a spoon.

What you need

2 **carrots**, finely chopped

2 eating **apples**, peeled, cored and chopped

200 g/7 oz **couscous**

250 ml/9 fl oz **vegetable stock**

1 tablespoon **sunflower oil**

1 **courgette**, diced

1 **red pepper**, diced

4 **spring onions**, roughly chopped

220 g/7¾ oz can **sweetcorn**, drained

50 g/1¾ oz **dried apricots**, roughly chopped

What to do

1. First, make a simple carrot and apple purée by steaming the carrot and apple for 8–10 minutes until tender. Use a hand blender to purée until smooth. Set aside.

2. Place the couscous in a bowl. In a small saucepan, bring the vegetable stock to the boil. Stir in 120 g/4¼ oz of the carrot and apple purée, then pour the mixture over the couscous and cover the bowl with clingfilm. Leave to stand for 5 minutes. (You can freeze any leftover purée for use another time.)

3. Meanwhile, heat the oil in a large frying pan and fry the remaining vegetables for 5 minutes until they have softened a little. Stir in the apricots and the couscous mixture and heat through.

4. Serve warm or cold. (You could even serve it warm with some spoonfuls of our Clever Tomato Sauce – see page 32 – for extra zing, if you like.)

Tuck-in tortilla toasties

serves **2** prep **10** minutes cook **5** minutes

Wrapping up lots of good stuff in a tortilla and then toasting it in a frying pan is a great way to use up leftovers and easy for little ones to hold in their hands to eat. Try out different fillings to get their taste buds tingling.

What you need

2 teaspoons **olive oil**, for brushing

2 **flour tortillas**

100 g / 3½ oz **Cheddar cheese**, grated

100 g/3½ oz **cooked chicken breast**, torn into small pieces

50 g/1¾ oz **ham**, roughly chopped

2 **spring onions**, trimmed and roughly chopped

2 **mushrooms**, thinly sliced

What to do

1. Lightly brush a large frying pan with oil. Lay a tortilla flat in the frying pan and arrange half the filling ingredients over half of it, keeping a clear 3 cm/1¼ inch edge. Fold the empty half of the tortilla over the top.

2. Heat the tortilla over a moderate heat for 2–3 minutes until the Cheddar starts to melt. Using 2 fish slices, carefully turn over the tortilla and cook for a further 2 minutes on the other side. Remove the frying pan from the heat and slide out the toasted tortilla onto a chopping board. Cut the tortilla into 3 wedges. Repeat with the other tortilla and remaining ingredients.

Pick me up!

Easy cheesy courgette frittata

Getting grated courgettes into these frittatas is a simple way to sneak some good-for-you greens into a meal. The frittata is delicious warm or cold and makes a great finger food.

What you need

6 **eggs**

250 g/9 oz **Cheddar cheese**, grated

250 g/9 oz **courgette**, coarsely grated

50 g/1¾ oz **raisins** (optional)

3 **spring onions** or 75 g/2½ oz **leek** or **white onion**, finely chopped

Small pinch of **chilli powder** or **cayenne pepper**

1 tablespoon **olive oil**

What to do

1. Preheat the grill to medium. Crack the eggs into a large bowl and beat well using a balloon whisk. Add the Cheddar, courgette and raisins (if using), the spring onions, leeks or white onion, and the chilli powder or cayenne pepper and beat again to combine.

2. Heat the oil in a 30 cm/12 inch frying pan, then pour in the egg mixture and cook over a gentle heat for 2–3 minutes until the base of the frittata is set. Place the frittata under the grill and cook for a further 3–4 minutes until the top is set and golden.

3. Slide the frittata out onto a plate and cut into 8 wedges. Serve warm or cold with salad.

Go crackers!

Can I help?

Little ones can have a go at cracking the eggs into the bowl and then take a turn at beating them with a fork or balloon whisk. Who has the fastest action?

Five ways with pitta, wrap or roll fillings

Bored with the same old sandwich fillings? These flavour and texture combinations put the brilliant back into bread – they are delicious, nutritious and, best of all, exciting.

Chompy cheese, carrot + apple

serves **2** prep **5** minutes

1 tablespoon unsweetened **apple sauce** or **apple purée**

75 g/2½ oz **cream cheese**

1 tablespoon **whole milk**

1 small **carrot**, grated

50 g/1¾ oz **Cheddar cheese**, grated

¼ eating **apple**, grated

2 **pitta breads**, toasted

If you're making your own apple purée, peel, core and chop 1 eating apple. Steam it until soft, then mash with a fork.

Blend the cream cheese with the milk, then fold in the apple sauce or 1 tablespoon of purée. Stir in the carrot, Cheddar and eating apple. Make a slit in the pittas and fill them with the cheese mixture. Cut each pitta in half to serve.

Fit-for-a-king coronation chicken with mango

serves **2** prep **5** minutes

2 tablespoons **mayonnaise**

2 tablespoons well-chopped **mango**

¼ teaspoon **medium curry powder**

150 g/5½ oz **cooked chicken breast**, torn into small pieces

50 g/1¾ oz **sultanas**

2 **flour tortillas**

2 small handfuls of **rocket**

Use a hand blender to combine the mayonnaise, mango and curry powder together, then stir in the chicken and sultanas.

Spoon half the mixture in a line across the centre of 1 tortilla, then scatter with half the rocket and roll up tightly. Repeat for the other tortilla.

Cut each tortilla in half to serve.

Crumbly feta + red grape

serves 2 | prep 5 minutes

50 g/1¾ oz **feta cheese**, crumbled

25 g/1 oz finely **chopped walnuts**

1 **celery stick**, finely chopped

50 g/1¾ oz **seedless red grapes**, halved or quartered

2 tablespoons **mayonnaise**

2 **pitta breads**, toasted

Fold all the filling ingredients together in a bowl until well combined.

Make a slit in the pittas and fill with the cheese mixture. Cut each pitta in half to serve.

Sunshine hummus with basil

serves 2 | prep 5 minutes

1 **clementine**, segmented and chopped

100 g/3½ oz **hummus**

1 small **carrot**, grated

1 tablespoon shredded **basil** leaves

2 **flour tortillas**

Mix all the filling ingredients together in a bowl until well combined.

Spoon half the mixture in a line across the centre of 1 tortilla and roll the tortilla up tightly. Repeat for the other tortilla.

Cut each tortilla in half to serve.

Terrific tuna tzatziki with green grapes

serves 2 | prep 5 minutes

200 g/7 oz can **tuna steak** in spring water, drained well

4 tablespoons **tzatziki**

50 g/1¾ oz **seedless green grapes**, halved or quartered

2 **wholemeal rolls**, halved

Mix all the filling ingredients together in a bowl until well combined.

Pile half the filling into each roll. Cut in half to serve.

Nibbly nacho feast

Children will love to dig in to this crunchy, gooey feast of flavour – all you need is fingers.

What you need

200 g/7 oz bag **tortilla chips**

75 g/2½ oz **mozzarella cheese**, grated

Lime wedges, to serve (optional)

For the tomato salsa

3 **tomatoes**, chopped

3 **spring onions**, finely sliced

Juice of ½ **lime** (reserve the other ½ lime for wedges, if using)

A handful of **coriander**, roughly chopped

½ teaspoon **smoked paprika**

For the avocado salsa (guacamole)

1 ripe **avocado**

1 tablespoon **sweet chilli dipping sauce**

What to do

1. Preheat the grill to high.

2. To make the tomato salsa, mix together the tomatoes, spring onions, lime juice, coriander and smoked paprika. Set aside.

3. To make the guacamole, mash the avocado flesh with the chilli sauce. Set aside.

4. Place the tortilla chips on a large heatproof platter and spoon over the tomato salsa, scatter with the cheese and place them under the preheated grill for 2–3 minutes until the cheese has melted.

5. Spoon the guacamole over the top and serve with lime wedges (if using).

Colour me in

Dee-licious dinners

How many different veggies can you name?
Can you get up to 10?

Love, Ella x

Hugely hearty four-bean feast

serves **2+4** adults + kids | prep **10** minutes | cook **35** minutes (omit green beans)

True to its name, this is a warming feast packed full of delicious flavour, heaps of veg and filling, nutritious beans. This is a good one to make for all the family to enjoy.

What you need

1 tablespoon **sunflower oil**

1 **onion**, chopped

1 **carrot**, diced

300 g/10½ oz **butternut squash**, cut into 1 cm/½ inch dice

400 g/14 oz can **red kidney beans**, drained and rinsed

400 g/14 oz can **cannellini beans**, drained and rinsed

400 g/14 oz can **haricot beans**, drained and rinsed

400 g/14 oz can **chopped tomatoes**

50 g/1¾ oz **green beans**, cut into quarters

150 ml/¼ pint **vegetable stock**

A handful of **basil** leaves, roughly torn

What to do

1. Preheat the oven to 200°C/400°F/Gas Mark 6.

2. Heat the oil in a large frying pan and fry the onion, carrot and squash for 5 minutes until the onion has softened.

3. Add all the canned beans, the tomatoes and the green beans, then add the vegetable stock and stir to combine. Transfer everything to a casserole dish, cover and bake for 30 minutes.

4. Stir in the basil and serve with couscous or mashed potatoes.

Tomorrow's lunch

If you have any of your delicious beany stew left over, keep it to spoon onto a hot baked potato, topped with a little cheese; or whiz it up to make a yummy lunchtime soup.

Can I help?

Bean prep

Once you've tipped the beans into a sieve to drain them, ask your little one to give you a hand rinsing them through – it's culinary water play!

Ella's dad's sweet + sour prawns

serves 6 | prep 15 minutes | cook 7 minutes

This recipe from the Lindley family kitchen is a great introduction to the sweet, tangy, savoury flavours used in recipes from all over Asia. We've cut the vegetables into strips, but you can slice them any way you like.

What you need

2 tablespoons **sunflower oil**

4 **spring onions**, sliced

1 **garlic** clove, sliced

225 g/8 oz **raw tiger prawns**

1 **red pepper**, halved, deseeded and sliced

12 **baby sweetcorn**, halved lengthways

2 **carrots**, cut into strips

2 **pineapple** rings, cut into chunks

For the sauce

1 tablespoon **light soy sauce**

1 tablespoon **white wine vinegar**

¼ **banana** and ¼ **mango**, mashed together

1 teaspoon **cornflour**

1 tablespoon **water**

1 tablespoon **ketchup**

1 teaspoon **sweet chilli dipping sauce**

What to do

1. First make the sauce: simply mix together all of the sauce ingredients in a bowl. Set aside.

2. Heat the oil in a wok or large frying pan and add the spring onions, garlic and prawns and fry them for 2 minutes over a medium heat, stirring continuously until the prawns are pink all over.

3. Add the pepper, baby sweetcorn and carrots and cook for a further 2–3 minutes until the vegetables are just soft.

4. Add the sauce and the pineapple chunks and stir everything together to combine well.

5. Cook for a further 1 minute until the sauce is bubbling and hot.

6. Serve immediately with noodles or rice.

That's magic!

Encourage your little one to watch the prawns change colour as they cook – as if by magic, their dull grey becomes beautiful pink.

Easy peasy veggie risotto

serves **4** prep **5** minutes cook **30** minutes

Risotto is so often a winning formula for tiny taste buds. This pea, leek and courgette version is especially easy to put together, but absolutely packed with green-food goodness.

What you need

1 **vegetable stock cube**

200 g/7 oz **easy-cook long grain rice**

75 g/2½ oz **frozen peas**, defrosted

1 tablespoon **olive oil**

1 **leek**, finely chopped

1 **courgette**, finely chopped

150 ml/¼ pint **carrot juice**

Cheddar cheese, grated, to serve

What to do

1. In a large saucepan bring 1 litre/1¾ pints of water to the boil. Crumble in the stock cube and add the rice. Bring the liquid back to the boil, then reduce the heat to low and simmer uncovered for 10–15 minutes until the rice is tender, adding the peas for the last 5 minutes.

2. Drain the rice and pea mixture and set aside.

3. Heat the oil in a large frying pan or wok and cook the leek and courgette for approximately 5 minutes, stirring occasionally, until softened.

4. Add the rice and pea mixture and stir well, then add the carrot juice and continue to cook for a further 2 minutes until piping hot.

5. Serve hot with some grated Cheddar sprinkled on top.

I love my greens!

Magical Moroccan-style chicken

serves 4 — prep 15 minutes — cook 25 minutes

This hotpot style dish packs in fruit, vegetables and legumes for an all-round nutritional boost. You could purée it and serve it with baby rice for very little ones.

What you need

1 tablespoon **sunflower oil**

2 **chicken breasts** (about 300 g/10½ oz), diced

1 large **carrot**, sliced

1 **leek**, sliced

1 **red pepper**, chopped

1 teaspoon **ground cumin**

½ teaspoon **ground cinnamon**

400 g/14 oz can **chickpeas**, drained and rinsed

1 tablespoon **tomato purée**

600 ml/1 pint **vegetable stock**

100 g/3½ oz **dried apricots**

50 g/1¾ oz **dried prunes**

A few **coriander leaves**, to serve (optional)

What to do

1. Heat the oil in a large saucepan and fry the chicken pieces for 4 minutes until golden on all sides. Add the vegetables and spices and fry for a further 2–3 minutes.

2. Add the chickpeas, tomato purée, vegetable stock, apricots and prunes and bring to the boil. Then reduce the heat to low, cover and simmer for 15–20 minutes, stirring occasionally, until all the ingredients are tender.

3. Serve on a bed of couscous sprinkled with the coriander leaves (if using).

Design your own fez

Tasty turkey + rice packed peppers

Cinnamon and raisins give these stuffed peppers a hint of Middle Eastern flavour. They are a great way to introduce little ones to sweet spices.

What you need

6 **red peppers**

75 g/2½ oz **brown rice**

350 g/12 oz **lean minced turkey**

1 small **onion**, chopped

400 g/14 oz can **chopped tomatoes**

3 tablespoons **tomato purée**

1 tablespoon **Worcestershire sauce**

50 g/1¾ oz **raisins**

½ teaspoon **ground cinnamon**

50 g/1¾ oz **mozzarella cheese**, finely chopped

What to do

1. Preheat the oven to 180°C/350°F/Gas Mark 4. Bring a large saucepan of water to the boil (use enough water to cover the peppers). Cut the tops from the peppers and discard them, then scoop out the core and seeds. Place the peppers into the boiling water, filling their cavities, and cook for 4 minutes until they begin to soften. Remove the peppers from the water using a slotted spoon (leave the water boiling) and set them aside to drain on kitchen paper, open-end down.

2. Add the rice to the water and cook for 20 minutes until tender.

3. Meanwhile, place the turkey and onion into a large heavy-based frying pan and cook over a high heat for 8–10 minutes, stirring and breaking up the turkey as much as possible. Add the tomatoes, tomato purée, Worcestershire sauce, raisins and cinnamon and stir well. Bring to the boil, then reduce the heat and cover and simmer for 5 minutes.

4. Drain the cooked rice, then stir into the mince mixture. Place the peppers, open-end up, into an ovenproof dish and fill each with with some of the mince mixture. Scatter over the mozzarella, then bake in the preheated oven for 15 minutes until the cheese is golden brown.

5 ways

Five ways with green vegetables

Greens don't have to be boring. We've found the perfect partners for green beans, sprouts, broccoli, spinach and courgettes – making the most of all the natural, fresh flavours. High 5 if your little ones try all 5!

Good-for-you green beans

serves 4 | prep 5 minutes | cook 8 minutes

300 g/10½ oz **fine green beans**, trimmed

2 tablespoons **olive oil**

3 **shallots**, finely chopped

50g/1¾ oz **pine nuts**

Cook the beans in boiling water for 5 minutes until just tender, then drain.

Meanwhile, heat the oil in a frying pan and fry the shallots for 2 minutes, add the pine nuts and fry for 1–2 minutes. Add the cooked beans and stir-fry for 2–3 minutes to heat through. Serve immediately.

Special sprouts

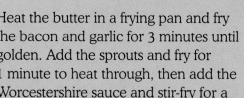

serves 4 | prep 5 minutes | cook 15 minutes

350 g/12 oz **Brussels sprouts**

Unsalted butter, for frying

75 g/2½ oz **unsmoked back bacon**, chopped

1 **garlic** clove, thinly sliced

1 teaspoon **Worcestershire sauce**

Cook the sprouts in boiling water for 10 minutes until just tender, then drain.

Heat the butter in a frying pan and fry the bacon and garlic for 3 minutes until golden. Add the sprouts and fry for 1 minute to heat through, then add the Worcestershire sauce and stir-fry for a few seconds before serving immediately.

Brilliant broccoli

300 g/10½ oz **broccoli florets**

1 tablespoon **toasted sesame oil**

1 tablespoon **sesame seeds**

1 tablespoon **light soy sauce**

Cook the broccoli in boiling water for 4–5 minutes until just tender, then drain.

Heat the oil in a frying pan and toast the sesame seeds for 1 minute until golden. Add the cooked broccoli and the soy sauce and stir-fry, tossing for 1 minute to heat through. Serve immediately.

Splendid spinach

1 kg/2 lb 4 oz bag **frozen spinach**

A pinch of **ground nutmeg**

4 tablespoons **crème fraîche**

1 tablespoon grated **Parmesan cheese**

Cook the spinach in a saucepan according to the packet instructions, drain and press out as much of the liquid as possible, then return the spinach to the pan.

Add the remaining ingredients and stir to combine. Serve immediately.

Cracking courgettes

1 tablespoon **olive oil**

450 g/1 lb **courgettes**, halved lengthways and sliced

Finely grated rind and juice of ½ **lemon**

A handful of **basil** leaves, finely chopped

Heat the oil in a frying pan and fry the courgettes for 5–6 minutes until golden and just tender.

Remove from the heat and stir in the lemon rind and juice and the basil. Serve immediately.

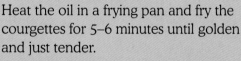

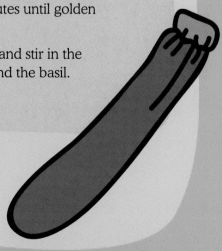

Kids' kedgeree

This yummy tea introduces kids to kedgeree without the need for the strong smoked-fish flavour and with only a little curry powder (fun for tiny taste buds).

What you need

350 g/12 oz **cod fillet**, skinned

300 ml/½ pint **whole milk**

50 g/1¾ oz **unsalted butter**

1 **onion**, finely chopped

½ teaspoon **cayenne pepper**

1 teaspoon **mild curry powder**

300 g/10½ oz **easy-cook long grain rice**

1 litre/1¾ pints **chicken stock** or water

150 g/5½ oz **frozen peas**, defrosted

150 g/5½ oz **frozen sweetcorn**, defrosted

4 **eggs**, hard-boiled and roughly chopped

2 tablespoons finely chopped **flat-leaf parsley**

What to do

1. Put the cod in a deep frying pan with the milk, bring to the boil, then reduce the heat to low and simmer uncovered for 5 minutes, or until cooked through.

2. Using a slotted spoon, transfer the fish to a bowl, reserving the warm milk. Flake the fish with a fork, taking care to remove any bones.

3. Melt the butter in a medium saucepan. Add the onion and cayenne pepper and cook for 2–3 minutes until the onion is beginning to soften. Add the curry powder and cook for a further 1 minute.

4. Add the rice and stir it to coat it in the oil. Pour in the chicken stock and the reserved milk and bring to the boil, then reduce the heat to low, cover and simmer for 10–15 minutes until the rice is cooked and almost all the stock and milk have been absorbed. Add the peas and the sweetcorn, stir thoroughly and cook for a further 2 minutes.

5. Carefully fold in the flaked fish and eggs. Sprinkle with the chopped parsley.

Ella's mum's easy chicken curry

serves 4 · prep 10 minutes · cook 30 minutes

Ella's mum first made this when Ella was just 3 years old – and Ella has been enjoying it ever since. It is a mild, sweet and creamy curry that's guaranteed to get tiny taste buds tingling with all the spices of exotic adventure.

What you need

2 tablespoons **olive oil**

1 small **onion**, chopped

2 **garlic** cloves, crushed

2 **chicken breasts** (about 300 g/10½ oz), cut into bite-sized pieces

2 cm/¾ inch piece **fresh ginger**, grated

1 teaspoon **mild curry powder**

1 small **sweet potato**, diced

250 g/9 oz **carrots**, sliced

250 ml/9 fl oz **coconut milk**

100 ml/3½ fl oz **vegetable stock**

1 small **mango**, cut into chunks

125 g/4½ oz **green beans**, trimmed

2 tablespoons finely chopped **flat-leaf parsley**

What to do

1) Heat the oil in a large saucepan and add the onion and garlic. Fry for 1 minute, stirring, then add the chicken pieces and cook for 3–4 minutes over a medium heat, stirring every now and then until the chicken pieces are golden brown all over.

2) Add the grated ginger and the curry powder and cook for a further 1 minute, stirring all the time. Add the sweet potato and carrots, then pour in the coconut milk and stock, and add the mango. Mix everything together well and bring the liquid to the boil. Cover, reduce the heat to low and simmer, stirring occasionally, for 20 minutes until the sweet potato is soft.

3) Add the beans and cook for a further 3 minutes until the beans are just soft. Finally, stir in the parsley. Serve immediately on a bed of rice or with a naan bread.

Ella's shortcut

To save some time on chopping, you can substitute the chunks of mango for 1 x 90g/3¼ oz pouch of Ella's Kitchen Smoothie Fruits – The Yellow One.

Colour me in

Big beef ragù

This recipe came from a man called Neil who works at Ella's Kitchen selling our food in lots of countries around the world. He calls it the 'perfect pasta partner' and it packs a big taste punch. Go easy on the chilli flakes for very little ones.

What you need

1 tablespoon **olive oil**

½ **onion**, roughly chopped

1 **garlic** clove, sliced

25 g/1 oz **unsmoked back bacon**, chopped

300 g/10½ oz **lean minced beef**

500 g/1 lb 2 oz **passata** or **Clever Tomato Sauce** (see page 32)

1 tablespoon **Worcestershire sauce**

1 teaspoon **fennel seeds**

A pinch of **chilli flakes**

A few **basil** leaves, to serve (optional)

Parmesan cheese, grated, to serve (optional)

What to do

1. Heat the oil in a large saucepan and cook the onion and garlic over a moderate heat for 3–4 minutes until beginning to soften. Add the bacon and cook for 3 minutes until opaque. Add the minced beef and cook for a further 5 minutes until the mince has browned.

2. Pour in the passata or Clever Tomato Sauce and 50 ml/2 fl oz of water. Add the Worcestershire sauce and the herbs and spices. Bring the sauce to the boil, then reduce the heat to low, cover and simmer for 10 minutes; then remove the lid and stir and cook for a further 8–10 minutes until the liquid has reduced by almost half.

3. Serve the ragù over cooked pasta and sprinkle with with basil leaves and freshly grated Parmesan (if using).

nee nar nee nar

Mega macaroni cheese

serves 2+2 adults + kids | prep 25 minutes | cook 35 minutes omit green beans

An easy twist on a family favourite, this dish is mega-tasty. The secret lies in the giant pasta tubes, which hold the delicious cheesiness so perfectly.

What you need

250 g/9 oz **large macaroni** or **penne pasta**, dried or fresh

50 g/1¾ oz **unsalted butter**

50 g/1¾ oz **plain flour**

600 ml/1 pint **whole milk**

200 g/7 oz **Cheddar cheese**, grated

1 teaspoon **English** or **Dijon mustard**

A pinch of **nutmeg**

100 g/3½ oz **unsmoked back bacon**, grilled and chopped into pieces

Draw something for the digger to carry

What to do

1. Preheat the oven to 190°C/375°F/Gas Mark 5. Bring a large saucepan of lightly salted water to the boil and cook the pasta according to the packet instructions. Drain and keep warm.

2. Meanwhile, melt the butter in a pan, add the flour, stir to combine and cook for 1 minute.

3. Gradually stir in the milk. Bring to the boil stirring continuously until the sauce thickens. Remove from the heat and stir in three-quarters of the Cheddar and add the mustard, nutmeg and bacon pieces. Add the pasta to the sauce and stir well.

4. Transfer the mixture to a large ovenproof dish and scatter with the remaining Cheddar.

5. Cook in the preheated oven for 20 minutes until golden.

6. Serve with green beans and a few grilled cherry tomatoes.

More veg!

Make your macaroni cheese more mega – try adding some of these veggies.

mmmmmmmmmmmmmacaroni

How does your fruit + veg grow?

Picking food out of the ground or off a tree helps children to get a proper sense of what food looks like before it arrives in the shops. Digging up potatoes makes for muddy fun; picking strawberries can turn fingers bright red. Scour your local paper and check online to see what pick-your-own possibilities there are near you.

1. Go prepared

Make a date for the whole family to go together. Take gloves, wet-wipes, wellies and even a change of clothes – this could get grubby! Some pick-your-own farms have family centres where children can learn about the produce or see some animals.

What to choose?

Think about what works well for you all. Little ones will love picking strawberries, raspberries and peas, which grow low to the ground. Older children may like reaching for apples or pears from big trees in an orchard.

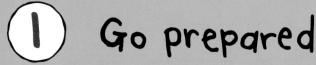

Pick + talk

While you pick, talk about everything you can feel, see and smell. What does the earth feel like? What about the leaves? Are the fruit or veg you're picking hard or soft? How are they different from what you buy in the shops? Do they have a different smell? Perhaps they even look different. Talk about big and small. For potatoes, onions and large fruit, count them as you put them in the basket.

Go to market

If you can't get picking, visit a farmers' market, where the produce is fresh, fresh, fresh!

Heads up!

After apple or potato picking, try making your own fruit and veg heads. Cut out 2 eyes, a nose and a mouth from a magazine and stick them on. Add some wool for hair or feathers to give feathery locks. Pom-poms with jewel stickers make gorgeous ears complete with earrings!

At home

Wash your booty together – who can scrub their potatoes cleanest? Taste the fruits as soon as you have washed them – deee-licious! Talk about your favourite ways to eat your hoard – then serve some of it up for tea. Yum!

Mmmmoussaka

serves **4** | prep **10** minutes | cook **50** minutes

Named after the sound little ones make when they eat it, this delicious dinner combines lamb mince with smooth sweet potato for a scrummy twist. Using crème fraîche instead of béchamel sauce saves you time without losing any creaminess.

What you need

2–3 tablespoons **olive oil**

½ **onion**, chopped (optional)

225 g/8 oz **lean minced lamb**

120 g/4¼ oz mashed **sweet potato**

1 small **aubergine**, sliced into rounds about 1 cm/½ in thick

1 large **potato**, sliced

100 g/3½ oz **Cheddar cheese**, grated

150 g/5½ oz **crème fraîche**

What to do

1. Preheat the oven to 200°C/400°F/Gas Mark 6.

2. Heat 1 tablespoon of the oil in a saucepan, add the onion (if using) and cook for 3 minutes over a medium heat until softened. Add the mince and cook for 4–5 minutes. Then, reduce the heat, add the sweet potato mash and cook for a further 1 minute. Remove from the heat; set aside.

3. Add the remaining oil to a large frying pan and gently fry the aubergine rounds for 10 minutes until soft.

4. Meanwhile, place the slices of potato in a large saucepan of water, bring to the boil, then reduce the heat to low and simmer uncovered for 10 minutes until the potatoes are slightly softened but not mushy.

5. In a shallow ovenproof dish, put a layer of meat mixture followed by a layer of both potato and aubergine. Repeat with the remaining ingredients, finishing with a neat layer of the potato and aubergine slices.

6. In a bowl mix three-quarters of the grated cheese with the crème fraîche. Spread this mixture over the top layer of the moussaka. Sprinkle over the remaining cheese, then cook in the oven for about 30 minutes until the top is golden and bubbling.

Blow!

Ella's shortcut

To save having to mash up a sweet potato, try using 1 x 120 g/4¼ oz pouch of Ella's Kitchen Sweet Potatoes, Pumpkin, Apples + Blueberries and you get the added benefit of fruity goodness, too!

73

Totally cool Caribbean chicken with mango + pineapple

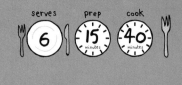

serves 6 | prep 15 minutes | cook 40 minutes

A flavour of the Caribbean makes this the most laid back of dinners. Watch it bring happy, sunny smiles to everyone at your table.

What you need

1 tablespoon **sunflower oil**

3 large **chicken breasts** (about 500 g/1 lb 2 oz), diced

1 **onion**, chopped

400 g/14 oz **potatoes**, diced

200 g/7 oz **butternut squash**, diced

1 teaspoon **medium curry powder**

½ teaspoon **ground cumin**

¼ teaspoon **ground cinnamon**

A pinch of **turmeric**

200 ml/7 fl oz **vegetable stock**

400 g/14 oz can **chopped tomatoes**

1 **mango**, chopped into small pieces

432 g/15¼ oz can **pineapple chunks** in natural juice, drained

What to do

1. Heat the oil in a large saucepan and fry the chicken and onion for 5 minutes until the onion is soft. Add the potato, squash and spices and cook for a further 4–5 minutes until the chicken is cooked through.

2. Add the vegetable stock and tomatoes to the pan and bring the sauce to the boil.

3. Stir in the chopped mango and the pineapple chunks, then reduce the heat to low, cover and simmer for 20 minutes, stirring occasionally. Remove the lid and cook for a further 10 minutes until the liquid has reduced to a thick sauce.

4. Serve immediately with rice.

Freeze!

This makes a brilliant dish for freezing so you can enjoy quick-fix Caribbean sunshine whatever the weather.

Zingy lamb + couscous with mangoes + raisins

serves 6 · prep 15 minutes · cook 1¾ hours

omit green beans

Packed full of flavoursome fruit and veg, this couscous dish really does zing!

What you need

2 tablespoons **olive oil**

1 **garlic** clove, crushed

350 g/12 oz **lamb leg fillet**, diced

1 **onion**, chopped

2 teaspoons **ground cumin**

½ teaspoon **ground cinnamon**

1 **carrot**, diced

350 g/12 oz **butternut squash**, diced

400 g/14 oz can **chopped tomatoes**

500 ml/17 fl oz **vegetable stock**

1 ripe **mango**, chopped into small pieces

100 g/3½ oz **green beans**, cut into 1 cm/½ inch pieces

200 g/7 oz **couscous**

100 g/3½ oz **raisins**

What to do

1. Preheat the oven to 180°C/350°F/Gas Mark 4.

2. Heat the oil in a frying pan and fry the garlic, lamb, onion and spices for 5 minutes until the lamb has browned on all sides. Transfer the mixture to a casserole dish.

3. Put the carrot and squash in the frying pan and cook for 3–4 minutes until softened, then add the tomatoes and 300 ml/½ pint of the stock and bring the mixture to the boil.

4. As soon as the tomato and stock mixture starts to boil, remove it from the heat and stir it into the lamb. Add the chopped mango, give it all another stir, then cover and bake in the oven for 1½ hours until the lamb is tender.

5. Once the lamb is ready, boil the green beans in the remaining stock for 2–3 minutes until just tender. Remove the beans from the liquid with a slotted spoon and set aside. Pour the stock into a measuring jug and set aside.

6. Put the couscous and raisins into a heatproof bowl and add the beans. Check how much stock you have in the measuring jug – you'll need 200 ml/7 fl oz, so top up the liquid with some boiling water if necessary. Pour the liquid over the couscous. Cover it with clingflim and leave it for 5 minutes until moist. Fluff the couscous with a fork and serve it with the lamb.

Cosy cottage pie

serves 6 · prep 20 minutes · cook 1 hour

omit peas

Homely and hearty – even if you don't live in a cottage – this is always a favourite with little and big ones alike.

What you need

600 g/1 lb 5 oz **potatoes**, diced

50 ml/2 fl oz **whole milk**

200 g/7 oz **sweet potato**, diced

1 **carrot**, diced

1 **onion**, chopped

500 g/1 lb 2 oz **lean minced beef**

½ teaspoon **ground cinnamon**

250 ml/9 fl oz **vegetable stock**

2 **tomatoes**, chopped

100 g/3½ oz **frozen peas**, defrosted

What to do

1. Preheat the oven to 200°C/400°F/Gas Mark 6.

2. Cook the potatoes in boiling water for 10–15 minutes or until tender. Drain them and return them to the saucepan. Pour in the milk, then mash the potatoes well.

3. While the potatoes are cooking, in another saucepan cook the sweet potato and carrot in boiling water for 10 minutes. Drain them and coarsely mash.

4. Fry the onion, minced beef and cinnamon in a large saucepan for 5 minutes until the mince is completely brown. Add the stock, the mashed sweet potato and carrot mixture and the tomatoes to the mince and cook for 5 minutes. Add the peas, give it a stir and transfer it all to an ovenproof serving dish. Top with the mashed potato and bake in the oven for 30 minutes until golden.

Ella's shortcut

To save on some chopping time, replace the sweet potato and carrots with 1 x 120 g/4¼ oz pouch of Ella's Kitchen Spinach, Apples + Swedes and reduce the amount of stock to 200 ml/7 fl oz.

Squishy salmon fishcakes

serves **2+2** adults + kids

prep **20** minutes + cooling

cook **25** minutes

omit green beans

Break out your artistic side and create lots of squishy fishy goodness with lots of squishy fishy style.

What you need

400 g/14 oz **potatoes**, cut into large dice

1 **carrot**, cut into small dice

200 g/7 oz **salmon fillets**, skin removed

3 tablespoons **sunflower oil**

1 small **leek**, thinly sliced

25 g/1 oz **green beans**, finely chopped

2 tablespoons finely chopped **flat-leaf parsley**

Blowing bubbles

Turn the plate into a work of art – ask your little one to arrange a few peas as if the fishy fishcakes were blowing bubbles.

What to do

1. Cook the potato and carrot in boiling water for 15 minutes until tender. Drain and mash them together, and set the mash aside to cool.

2. Meanwhile, poach the salmon in simmering water for 5 minutes until cooked through, then allow to cool. Break up the fish into flakes, taking care to ensure that there are no bones.

3. Heat 1 tablespoon of the oil in a large frying pan and fry the leek and beans for 5 minutes until tender. Stir them into the carrot and potato mash, then add the cooked salmon and the parsley to the mixture and stir again.

4. Using your hands, mould the mixture into 2 large fishcakes and 2 smaller fishcakes. (Fishy shapes look great.)

5. Heat the remaining oil in a frying pan and cook the fishcakes for 5 minutes, turning once, until golden on both sides and warm through. Serve immediately with some peas.

Colour us in

Punchy pork hotpot with apples

serves 6 | prep 15 minutes | cook 2¼ hours

omit green beans

Pork and apples always make a scrummy combination and this full-of-flavour dish is no exception. It's perfect for a warming tea.

What you need

2 tablespoons **sunflower oil**

400 g/14 oz **pork loin**, diced

600 g/1 lb 5 oz **potatoes**, thinly sliced

1 **onion**, sliced

2 **carrots**, sliced

1 **leek**, sliced

1 **garlic** clove, crushed

1 teaspoon **dried mixed herbs**

50 g/1¾ oz **green beans**, halved

1 eating **apple**, cored and sliced

300 ml/½ pint **vegetable stock**

What to do

1. Preheat the oven to 180°C/350°F/Gas Mark 4.

2. Heat 1 tablespoon of the oil in a frying pan, add the pork and cook for about 5 minutes, turning occasionally until the meat has browned on all sides.

3. Meanwhile, use half of the sliced potatoes to make a thin potato layer in the base of a casserole dish. Spoon the browned pork on top.

4. In the same frying pan, heat the remaining 1 tablespoon of oil and fry the onion, carrots, leek, garlic and herbs for 5 minutes, until the onion, leek and garlic are soft.

5. Spoon the vegetables over the top of the pork and then sprinkle over the beans. Top with a layer of sliced apple and finally the remaining sliced potatoes. Pour the vegetable stock over the top. Cover the casserole and bake the hotpot in the oven for 1¾ hours. Remove the lid and continue to bake for a further 15 minutes, or until the potatoes are golden.

Can I help?

Layer patterns

Ask your little helpers to make the layers of potato and apple in the hotpot – can they make a pattern with the slices?

Ella's shortcut

If you want to save some time, replace the apple slices with 1 x 70 g/2½ oz pouch of Ella's Kitchen Apples, Apples, Apples. Stir it into the vegetable mixture.

Oink

Wonderfully warming fruity beef stew

serves 6 | prep 25 minutes | cook 2¼ hours

This is another of Ella's favourite meals – from her mum. Adding jam to the stew gives it a really fruity, tasty punch.

What you need

2 tablespoons **olive oil**

750 g/1 lb 10 oz **diced stewing beef**

1 **onion**, thinly sliced

300 g/10½ oz **carrots**, sliced

2 **plums** or **apricots**, stoned and sliced

1 **garlic** clove, crushed

1 tablespoon **tomato purée**

2 tablespoons **plain flour**

Finely grated rind of 1 **lemon**, plus 1 tablespoon of the juice

750 ml/1¼ pints **beef stock**

150 g/5½ oz **plum** or **damson jam**

Freshly ground **black pepper**

What to do

1. Preheat the oven to 160°C/315°F/Gas Mark 2–3.

2. Heat the oil in a large casserole. In batches, add the beef and cook for 3–4 minutes until browned on all sides. Remove each batch with a slotted spoon and set aside.

3. Add the onion to the casserole and cook for 2 minutes until softened. Add the carrots, plums or apricots, garlic, tomato purée and flour and cook for a further 2 minutes.

4. Return the browned beef and all its juices to the casserole along with the lemon rind and juice, the beef stock and the jam. Season with the pepper and bring to a simmer.

5. Cover and cook in the oven for 2 hours until the beef is tender. Serve with pasta or mashed potato.

Spoon skills

Can I help?

Even very little ones like to show their skills with a spoon or fork. Ask your toddler to give you a hand spooning in the jam at the end of the method. If they get sticky fingers? All the better to lick!

Scrummy salmon + veg parcels

makes **4** parcels · prep **10** minutes · cook **30** minutes

This is a fun way to cook simple, fresh ingredients. Wrapping the ingredients in shiny foil parcels makes them seem extra-special.

What you need

Olive oil, for drizzling

300 g/10½ oz **new potatoes**, thickly sliced, skin on

100 g/3½ oz **broccoli**, trimmed and halved

1 **red pepper**, cut into thick strips

6 **baby sweetcorn**, halved lengthways

½ teaspoon **dried mixed herbs**

2 tablespoons **sun-dried tomato purée**

4 **salmon fillets**, skin removed

What to do

1. Preheat the oven to 200°C/400°F/Gas Mark 6.

2. Drizzle 4 large squares of aluminium foil with a little olive oil and make a small pile of the vegetable ingredients in the centre of each. Sprinkle each pile with some of the herbs.

3. Spread a ½ tablespoon of the tomato purée over each of the salmon fillets. Place 1 fillet on top of each pile of vegetables. Scrunch up the foil pieces, leaving a small gap in the top of each parcel to let the steam escape. Place the parcels on a baking sheet and bake in the oven for 30 minutes until the vegetables are tender and the salmon is cooked through.

Go pesto!

Pesto (try our Green Pasta Sauce on page 96) makes a delicious alternative to the sun-dried tomato purée.

Foil scrunch-up

Can I help?

Your children will love helping you construct the parcels – especially when it comes to scrunching up that noisy foil. Marvel together at how the contents have miraculously transformed when the parcels come out of the oven.

5 ways

Five ways with potatoes

Who knew potatoes could be so tasty? Gone are the days of bland school mash. Encourage little ones to make shapes from the potato peelings – or see who can peel the longest strip (under supervision, of course).

Rosemary roasties

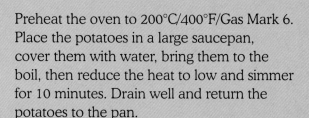
serves 6 · prep 10 minutes · cook 1 hour

700 g/1 lb 9 oz **King Edward potatoes**, cut into large chunks

3 tablespoons **sunflower oil**

1 tablespoon **rosemary** leaves

Preheat the oven to 200°C/400°F/Gas Mark 6. Place the potatoes in a large saucepan, cover them with water, bring them to the boil, then reduce the heat to low and simmer for 10 minutes. Drain well and return the potatoes to the pan.

Add the oil and shake the pan a little to coat the potato cubes. Transfer them to a baking sheet, drizzle over any excess oil left in the pan and sprinkle over the rosemary. Bake in the oven for 45–55 minutes until golden and crispy, turning the chunks after 30 minutes to make sure they go crispy all over.

Herby mash up

serves 6 · prep 10 minutes · cook 15 minutes

700 g/1 lb 9 oz **floury potatoes**, cut into chunks

50 g/1¾ oz **unsalted butter**

2 **garlic** cloves, crushed

50 ml/2 fl oz **whole milk**

2 tablespoons finely chopped **flat-leaf parsley**, or 2 tablespoons chopped **chives** and 4 tablespoons **crème fraîche** (optional)

Put the potatoes in a large saucepan, cover them with water, bring them to the boil, then reduce the heat to low and simmer for 10–15 minutes until tender, then drain.

Put the empty pan back on the heat. Melt the butter and add the garlic, then fry it for 1 minute until soft. Remove the pan from the heat. Add the potatoes and the milk and mash well, then stir in the parsley.

Alternatively, mash the potatoes with the milk and stir in the crème fraîche and chopped chives in place of the parsley.

Baby jackets

serves 6 | prep 2 minutes | cook 45 minutes

700 g/1 lb 9 oz **new potatoes**

1 tablespoon **olive oil**

Preheat the oven to 200°C/400°F/Gas Mark 6.

Place the potatoes on a baking sheet and sprinkle over the oil. Toss to coat evenly. Bake for 45 minutes or until golden and cooked all the way through.

Sweet potato fishy chips

serves 6 | prep 5 minutes | cook 30 minutes

700 g/1 lb 9 oz **sweet potatoes**, cut into thick slices

1 tablespoon **sunflower oil**

2 tablespoons **maple syrup**

Preheat the oven to 200°C/400°F/ Gas Mark 6. Use a fish-shaped cutter to cut your sweet-potato slices into fishy chips. Put them in a large roasting tin, add the oil and maple syrup and toss to coat. Spread the chips out on a baking sheet and bake for 25–30 minutes until tender, turning once.

Cheesy chips

serves 6 | prep 2 minutes | cook 25 minutes

700 g/1 lb 9 oz **oven chips**

75 g/2½ oz **Cheddar cheese**, grated

Preheat the oven to 220°C/425°F/ Gas Mark 7. Spread the chips out on a large baking tray and cook for 20–25 minutes or according to the packet instructions, until golden. Sprinkle over the Cheddar. Toss well until the cheese has melted slightly, then return to the oven for 1 minute.

Teeny-weeny turkey burger bites

makes 6 | prep 35 minutes + proving | cook 20 minutes

These teeny-weeny turkey burgers are beautifully lean and just right for little hands to hold. If you can't find turkey mince, chicken mince will work just as well. We made our own rolls using pizza-base mix, but use shop-bought mini-burger rolls if you're short of time.

What you need

150 g/5½ oz **lean turkey mince**

30 g/1 oz fresh **white breadcrumbs**

2 **egg yolks**

A large pinch of **dried mixed herbs** or 2 teaspoons finely chopped fresh **oregano**

A splash of **Worcestershire sauce** (optional)

Freshly ground **black pepper** (optional)

2 teaspoons **vegetable oil**

Slices of **tomato** and **cucumber**, to serve (optional)

For the rolls

1 x 145 g packet **pizza-base mix**

1 **egg**, beaten

Sesame seeds, for sprinkling

What to do

1) Preheat the oven to 220°C/425°F/Gas Mark 7. To make your mini rolls, make the pizza dough according to the packet instructions. Mould it into 6 ping-pong ball sized rolls. Cover these with a damp cloth and prove them for 30 minutes, or until they have doubled in size. Place the rolls on a baking sheet and put them in the oven for 10 minutes, until they sound hollow when you tap the base. Remove them from the oven, brush them with the beaten egg, sprinkle over the sesame seeds and return to the oven for 2–3 minutes until they are golden on top.

2) While the rolls are cooking, make the burgers. Mix the mince, breadcrumbs, egg yolk, herbs and Worcestershire sauce (if using) together in a bowl with a little freshly ground black pepper (if using), until the mixture is fully combined and moist, but holds together.

3) Divide the mixture into 6 equal portions, then flour your hands and roll each portion into a ball and gently flatten it into a burger shape.

4) Brush a nonstick frying pan with the oil, then put it on a low–medium heat and fry the burgers for 8–10 minutes, turning once, until they are completely cooked through.

5) Serve immediately in a mini-burger bun topped and tailed with a slice of cucumber and a slice of tomato (if using).

Bite me

Quick quesadillas

Eat like a Mexican. We think these delicious quesadillas provide a perfect opportunity for a fiesta atmosphere – how about giving out some moustaches and party whistles?

What you need

1 tablespoon **olive oil**

1 **chicken breast** (about 150 g/5½ oz), sliced into strips

½ **red pepper**, cut into thin strips

2 teaspoons **balsamic vinegar**

2 **flour tortillas**

1 tablespoon finely chopped **coriander**

50g/1¾ oz **Emmental** or **Cheddar cheese**, grated

What to do

1. Heat the oil in a frying pan and fry the chicken and pepper for 3–4 minutes, adding the balsamic vinegar for the final 1 minute of cooking, until the chicken is cooked through and the pepper is soft.

2. In a separate frying pan, lay a flour tortilla in the base of the pan and top with the cooked chicken and pepper, and the coriander. Sprinkle over the Emmental or Cheddar and top with the other tortilla.

3. Cover the pan with a lid and cook over a gentle heat for 12 minutes, or until the base of the tortilla is golden. Flip the tortilla over in the pan (you'll need 2 fish slices for this), and cook it for a further 1–2 minutes until the base is golden and the cheese has melted. Remove the tortilla from the pan and slice it into wedges.

4. Allow to cool slightly before serving.

Slurp me

Marvellous meatballs

makes **24** | prep **10** minutes | cook **20** minutes

This basic mixture will make handfuls of meatballs that are ideal for play-date dinners. We've served them here with our Clever Tomato Sauce, but they're delicious inside our Pizza Pocket Bites (see page 153), too.

What you need

3 tablespoons **apple purée**

25 g/1 oz **breadcrumbs**

2 tablespoons finely chopped **sage** leaves

500 g/1 lb 2 oz **lean minced pork**

½ teaspoon **ground nutmeg**

1 tablespoon **vegetable oil**

Freeze!

If you aren't using all the meatballs at once, you can freeze them (uncooked, or cooked and then cooled completely) for up to a month.

Ella's shortcut

If you don't want to spend time making the apple purée, you can substitute the same amount of Ella's Kitchen Apples, Apples, Apples instead.

What to do

1. To make the apple purée, peel, core and chop 2 eating apples. Steam until soft, then mash with a fork. (Freeze any leftover purée.)

2. Place the breadcrumbs and sage in a large bowl and add 50 ml/2 fl oz of boiling water. Allow the mixture to soak for 2–3 minutes, until the water has been absorbed and the mixture is cool enough to handle.

3. Add the pork, apple purée and nutmeg and use your hands to mix together the ingredients until fully combined and stiff. Mould the mixture into 24 mini meatballs.

4. Heat the oil in a large frying pan and fry the meatballs over a low heat for 15 minutes, turning occasionally, until cooked through. (You may need to do this in batches, in which case set each batch aside on a warm plate.)

5. Serve the meatballs on a mound of spaghetti topped with lashings of our Clever Tomato Sauce (see page 32).

Three easy pasta sauces

We asked kids what their favourite pasta sauces were. Red, green and white were the most popular replies! Whatever your child's favourite, these 3 sauces are packed full of good tasty stuff and work stirred into any shape, size or colour of pasta.

Red pasta sauce

serves 6 | prep 5 minutes | cook 17 minutes

1 tablespoon **sunflower oil**

1 **onion**, chopped

200 g/7 oz **unsmoked back bacon**, chopped

2 teaspoons **paprika**

700 g/1 lb 9 oz **tomatoes**, roughly chopped

150 ml/¼ pint **vegetable stock**

2 tablespoons finely chopped **flat-leaf parsley**

1. Heat the oil in a large saucepan and fry the onion and bacon for 4–5 minutes. Add the paprika and tomatoes and cook for 5 minutes.

2. Add the stock to the tomatoes, and simmer uncovered for 5–7 minutes. Stir in the parsley.

Green pasta sauce

serves 6 | prep 5 minutes | cook 3 minutes

5 tablespoons **extra-virgin olive oil**

2 **garlic** cloves, roughly chopped

100 g/3½ oz **pine nuts**

50 g/1¾ oz **basil**

50 g/1¾ oz **Parmesan cheese**, grated

1. Heat 1 tablespoon of the oil in a small frying pan and fry the garlic and pine nuts for 2–3 minutes until they turn golden.

2. Place the basil in a food processor and blitz to coarsely chop, add the pine-nut mixture, remaining oil, Parmesan and 100 ml/3½ fl oz of water. Process to give a coarse paste.

White pasta sauce

serves 6 | prep 5 minutes | cook 6 minutes

50 g/1¾ oz **unsalted butter**

50 g/1¾ oz **plain flour**

500 ml/17 fl oz **whole milk**

100 g/3½ oz **green beans**, cut into 1 cm/½ inch pieces

2 x 200 g/7 oz cans **tuna in springwater**, drained

50 g/1¾ oz **pitted black olives**, sliced

50 g/1¾ oz **Cheddar cheese**, grated

1 tablespoon finely chopped **chives**

1. Melt the butter in a saucepan and stir in the flour. Cook for 1 minute, then gradually add the milk. Add the beans and bring to the boil, stirring until thickened. Simmer for 3–4 minutes, or until the beans are tender.

2. Stir in the tuna, olives and Cheddar and cook for 1 minute to melt the cheese. Stir in the chives.

Lovely lasagne

So many mums tell us that they avoid making lasagne because it takes so long to prepare. This version (and its veggie alternative) will take you only 20 minutes – easy peasy. Why not cook up a big batch and freeze it in portions?

What you need

1 **onion**, chopped

500 g/1 lb 2 oz **lean minced beef**

1 **carrot**, diced

200 g/7 oz **mushrooms**, sliced

1 teaspoon **dried mixed herbs**

½ teaspoon grated **nutmeg**

400 g/14 oz can **chopped tomatoes**

6 dried **lasagne sheets**

1 **egg**, beaten

200 g/7 oz **crème fraîche**

50 g/1¾ oz **Cheddar cheese**, grated

Go veggie

For a vegetarian option, fry the onion and carrot as in the meat version, then add 1 diced aubergine, 1 diced courgette and 150 ml/¼ pint vegetable stock. Add the mushrooms, herbs, nutmeg and tomatoes, cover the pan and simmer for 10 minutes, stirring occasionally. Continue as for the meat recipe from step 3 onwards.

What to do

1. Preheat the oven to 200°C/400°F/Gas Mark 6.

2. Fry the onion, mince and carrot in a large saucepan for 2–3 minutes until the mince is brown. Stir in the mushrooms, herbs, nutmeg, tomatoes and 150 ml/¼ pint water. Bring the sauce to the boil, then reduce the heat to low and simmer, covered, for 10 minutes, stirring occasionally.

3. Meanwhile, cook the lasagne sheets in boiling water for 5–6 minutes, drain, then cool.

4. Mix the egg with the crème fraîche.

5. Place a third of the mince mixture in the base of a shallow ovenproof dish, then make a layer with 2 lasagne sheets and spoon over another third of the mince. Top with another 2 lasagne sheets and then the remaining third of the mince mixture. Layer on the remaining lasagne sheets and pour over the crème fraîche and egg mixture. Finally, sprinkle over the Cheddar and bake in the oven for 30–35 minutes until the top is golden.

6. Serve warm with a salad.

Can I help?

Layer it up

Parboiled lasagne sheets should be fairly robust for little hands to handle, so ask your toddler to help you make the pasta layers: you do the meat and he or she does the lasagne. This way lasagne making is a team effort!

Cool kiddie café

Children love to play at being grown-ups and what better way than to set up their own outdoor café in the garden. This is a great play-date activity, or a lovely way to involve the whole family in playing together. Of course, you can move the café inside on rainy days.

Make a menu

★ menu ★

Get creative with your menu. Find some paper, pens, stickers, glue and cut-outs of food from magazines and create a mouthwatering list of items that are on sale at your café. Don't forget the tea, coffee and juices, too. If you have a wipe-clean drawing board or blackboard you can create a specials list – let your little ones set the prices.

Pretend pizza

Try making pretend pizza slices out of cardboard – use differently coloured tissue paper for the toppings and cotton wool as melty cheese. If your customers demand pasta – no problem! Use a ball of yellow wool to make a bowl of delicious noodles.

② Lay the table

Find a brightly coloured blanket or sheet to use as a tablecloth. If you don't have an outdoor table, make this a picnic café and lay your tablecloth on the ground, using cushions for seats. Are there any flowers you could pick in the garden to put in a little cup in the middle of the table? Give them a sniff – do they smell beautiful? Don't forget the plastic knives and forks and some tea-set cups and saucers.

③ Gather your food

Use playdough to make cakes or pretend sandwiches for your café; while grass from the garden can make a pretend salad. You could also use real fruit, as well as water for tea and coffee.

④ Play your roles

Decide which of you will be the waiters, who will be the customers, and who will pretend to be the chef. Find aprons for the waiters and chef (who might need a hat, too, if you have one) and don't forget pen and paper to take orders. Show your customers to their seats and hand them their menus. What do the customers think of the food?

Teatime treat

When the game is over, keep the outdoor café and serve up proper tea there for your little ones. They will love it when you are the waiter or waitress serving real food in their café – will they leave you a tip?!

Full-of-sunshine Thai curry

Bursting with bright colours, this gentle introduction to Thai flavours provides plenty of adventure for tiny taste buds.

What you need

1 tablespoon **vegetable oil**

400 g/14 oz **butternut squash**, diced

1 large **onion**, diced

1 **carrot**, sliced

1 **red pepper**, sliced

100 g/3½ oz **sugar snap peas**

3 cm/1¼ inch piece **root ginger**, grated

1 **garlic** clove, crushed

1 teaspoon **ground cumin**

½ teaspoon **mild chilli powder**

400 ml/14 fl oz can **coconut milk**

1 **vegetable stock cube**, crumbled

A large handful of **coriander**, finely chopped

4 **lime** wedges, to serve (optional)

What to do

1. Heat the oil in a large frying pan and cook the squash, onion and carrot for 5 minutes unil the onion is soft. Add the pepper, sugar snap peas, ginger, garlic and spices and fry for 2–3 minutes, stirring occasionally.

2. Stir in the coconut milk and crumbled stock cube, cover and simmer for 10 minutes, stirring occasionally, until the vegetables are tender. Stir in the coriander.

3. Serve the curry with basmati rice, and lime wedges (if using).

Thai-taste-tastic!

Thai food is famously fragrant, which makes this a fab meal for encouraging your toddler to explore how smell and taste work together. Offer up the cut ginger root and a few coriander leaves for a sniff-fest. Talk about the different smells. Can your toddler taste those smells when he or she tucks into the bowl of cooked curry?

Chick-chick chicken pasta bake

Inspired by the Dale family – mum and dad work at Ella's making sure all our food is safe to eat – this comforting pasta dish is easy to make and topped with cheesy breadcrumbs.

What you need

450 g/1 lb **butternut squash**, diced

1 **carrot**, diced

1 teaspoon **olive oil**

1 **chicken breast** (about 150 g/5½ oz), diced

100 g/3½ oz **mushrooms**, finely sliced

80 ml/2½ fl oz **whole milk**

100 g/3½ oz small **pasta** shapes, such as pasta shells

1 thick slice of **farmhouse bread**

25 g/1 oz **Cheddar cheese**, grated

Ella's shortcut

If you don't want to purée the squash for this recipe, you can substitute it with 1 x 120 g/4¼ oz pouch of Ella's Kitchen Butternut Squash, Carrots, Apples + Prunes instead.

What to do

1. Preheat the oven to 200°C/400°F/Gas Mark 6.

2. Steam the butternut squash and carrot pieces for 10 minutes until tender, then blitz them together with a hand blender until you have a soft purée.

3. Heat the oil in a medium saucepan and add the chicken pieces. Fry the chicken for 10 minutes, turning occasionally, until cooked through, then add the mushrooms and cook for a further 4–5 minutes. Stir in 120 g/4¼ oz of the butternut squash and carrot purée (freeze any you have left over), then add the milk, stir, and cook for a further 1 minute. Remove the mixture from the heat.

4. Meanwhile, cook the pasta according to the packet instructions until al dente. Drain, and then add the pasta to the chicken mixture and mix together thoroughly. Transfer everything to a small, shallow ovenproof dish.

5. Using a food processor, blitz the bread into breadcrumbs, then place them in a bowl and stir through the grated Cheddar. Spoon the cheesy breadcrumb mixture over the pasta bake and cook in the oven for 20 minutes until the top is golden and crispy.

Perfect puds

Have you tried
the Swirly Whirly
Cheesecake?
It's my favourite!

Love, Ella x

Baby baked apples

When these come out of the oven, a gooey, sticky sauce will have appeared as if by magic.

What you need

8 mini eating **apples**

50 g/1¾ oz **unsalted butter**

50 g/1¾ oz **brown sugar**

1 teaspoon **ground cinnamon**

50 g/1¾ oz **raisins**

Juice of ½ **orange**

Squeeeeezy juicy

Whether you have a citrus press or a hand citrus juicer, pressing down on the flesh of the orange and watching the delicious juice come out is pure culinary magic for little ones. Put the juice in a measuring jug to see how much you managed to squeeze out.

What to do

1. Preheat the oven to 180°C/350°F/ Gas Mark 4. Wash and dry the apples. Cut a triangular-shaped cavity from each, removing most of the core at the same time, but keeping the bottom of the apple intact. Place the apples in a baking dish.

2. Mix together the butter and sugar, then stir in the cinnamon and raisins. Fill each of the apples with the cinnamon and raisin butter, then drizzle them with orange juice.

3. Place the apples in a baking dish and bake them for 40 minutes until soft and beginning to turn golden. Serve with spoonfuls of crème fraîche or Greek yogurt.

Scrummy

What shapes can you make?

Toasty, fruity brioche

serves 6 | prep 10 minutes | cook 20 minutes

Orange-coloured fruit such as peaches, mangoes and apricots – fresh or tinned – work best for this scrummy dessert. Serve it plain or with Greek yogurt or crème fraîche. If you prefer, you can swap the brioche for croissants.

What you need

6 slices **brioche**

25 g/1 oz **unsalted butter**, softened

2 tablespoons **apricot jam**

1 **mango**, or 6 **apricots** or 2 **nectarines** or 2 **peaches** or a mixture of any, stoned and sliced

1 tablespoon **soft brown sugar**

4 tablespoons freshly squeezed **orange juice**

What to do

1. Preheat the oven to 200°C/400°F/Gas Mark 6. Butter each slice of brioche, then place the slices into a baking dish so that they fit snugly and spread them with the apricot jam.

2. Place the sliced fruit on top of the brioche until the brioche is completely covered and you have used up all the fruit.

3. Sprinkle over the sugar and drizzle over the orange juice so that the brioche is moist.

4. Bake the pudding in the oven for 20 minutes until the brioche is slightly crisped and browned at the edges. Serve hot.

Fruity fun

Can I help?

In creating this recipe, the children can have all the creative fun – putting the fruit on top of the jammy brioche slices and making a pattern on top. Lay out the slices of fruit for them and away they go!

Colour me in

111

Big banana + honey dream

serves **6** prep **5** minutes

A match made in heaven, banana and honey make a dreamy combination that wraps a warm hug around the taste buds.

What you need

150 ml/¼ pint **whipping cream**

3 ripe **bananas**

250 ml/9 fl oz **Greek yogurt**

2 tablespoons **clear honey**

1 tablespoon **lemon juice**

Chocolate buttons or juicy **mango** slices, to decorate

What to do

1. Whip the cream until soft peaks form. Mash the bananas on a plate and then transfer them to a bowl.

2. Stir the yogurt, honey and lemon juice into the banana, then gently fold in the whipped cream.

3. Spoon the mixture into 6 individual serving dishes and decorate with the chocolate buttons or mango slices.

Causing a stir

Can I help?

Tiny tots will love having a turn at whipping the cream and stirring the mixture all together. Chocolate buttons or mango – the results are always irresistible!

Perfect pear + raspberry oaty crumble

serves 2+2 adults + kids

prep 15 minutes

cook 55 minutes omit hazelnuts

Making crumble is so much fun for little hands, and pears and raspberries are among the most perfect sweet crumble partners. This scrummy pud definitely rounds off a family Sunday roast.

What you need

50 g/1¾ oz **sugar**

3 **large pears**, or 400 g/14 oz **canned pears**, drained

150 g/5½ oz **raspberries**

For the crumble topping

250 g/9 oz **plain flour**

125 g/4½ oz **unsalted butter**

100 g/3½ oz **soft light brown sugar**

50 g/1¾ oz **porridge oats**

50 g/1¾ oz chopped **hazelnuts** (optional)

Crumbly fingers

Can I help?

Encourage your toddler to rub the crumble mixture gently between his or her fingertips – see if they can make it look like rain as it patters into the bowl.

What to do

1. Preheat the oven to 180°C/350°F/Gas Mark 4.

2. If you're using fresh pears, put the sugar into a large saucepan with 1 litre/1¾ pints of water. Place the pears in the pan. Bring up to a simmer and poach the pears for 20 minutes, until cooked through and tender. Drain them and allow to sit until they are cool enough to handle, then cut in half and remove the cores.

3. Slice the poached pears lengthways. Place them in a 1 litre/1¾ pint ovenproof dish. If you're using canned pears, roughly chop them and put them into the dish. Add the raspberries and toss everything together.

4. To make the topping, put the flour into a bowl and add the butter. Rub the butter into the flour with your fingertips until it resembles breadcrumbs. Stir in the sugar and the porridge oats, and the hazelnuts (if using).

5. Spread the crumble mixture onto a baking sheet and place it in the oven for 10 minutes. This will give you a lovely crunchy crumble topping. Remove it from the oven and sprinkle it over the fruit. Cook the crumble for 25 minutes until golden. Serve warm with custard, vanilla ice cream or crème fraîche.

Pour me over

Eat me before I melt

The melty one

serves 8 | prep 10 minutes | cook 4–5 minutes

This healthy variation on a traditional baked Alaska uses frozen yogurt instead of ice cream. Tuck in quickly to experience the hot and cold sensation.

What you need

3 **egg whites**

75 g/2½ oz **caster sugar**

¼ teaspoon **cream of tartar**

2–3 scoops **frozen fruit yogurt** (strawberry or raspberry works best)

1 shop-bought **Madeira cake**, cut in half (or make your own, see below)

Make your cake

If you have time, why not make your own Madeira cake? Preheat the oven to 160°C/315°F/ Gas Mark 3. Cream together 175 g/6 oz unsalted butter and 175 g/6 oz caster sugar in a bowl, then beat in 3 lightly beaten large eggs a little at a time. Sift in 250 g/ 9 oz self-raising flour and fold it in, followed by the juice and finely grated rind of a lemon. Place the mixture in a parchment-lined 900 g/2 lb loaf tin and bake it in the middle of the oven for 40–50 minutes until it is golden brown on top and a skewer inserted in the centre comes out clean.

What to do

1. Preheat the oven to 220°C/425°F/Gas Mark 7.

2. Place the egg whites in a medium-sized bowl and whisk them until the mixture forms peaks. Add the cream of tartar and whisk again for a further 1 minute.

3. Add the sugar a little at a time, whisking well after each addition, to make a meringue.

4. Place the cake on a baking sheet, with the 2 halves next to each other.

5. Place the scoops of frozen yogurt on top of the cake, keeping a 3 cm/1¼ inch rim around the yogurt.

6. Coat the entire cake and frozen yogurt in the meringue, taking care to leave no gaps.

7. Bake the pudding in the oven for 4–5 minutes until the meringue begins to turn golden.

8. Remove the baking sheet from the oven and serve the pudding immediately with a few pieces of fresh fruit to complement the yogurt flavour, if you wish.

Playing shops

Creating your own shop together is a perfect opportunity for play involving all 5 senses. A greengrocer's shop is a great way to start – and will fire your children's imaginations to think about the fruit and veg they so often see at mealtimes. Keep it varied by using different 'goods' each time you play.

① Make your signage

Every shop needs an open and closed sign. Grab some card (the inside of an old cereal box will do) and get creative. You can write the word, but let the little hands do the decorating.

Make a kiosk

Take a large cardboard box (big enough for a little face to appear in), then using a craft knife cut a flap for the shop window where goods and play cash change hands. Together, decorate the outside of the kiosk with lettering and stickers and make a sign that says 'Pay here'.

(2) Choose your stock

It's time to raid the fridge! Borrow a few tomatoes, carrots and onions, and any other vegetables that your toddler wants you to sell in the store. Don't forget the fruit and herbs, too. Talk about the colours, smells and textures. Remember to get out the weighing scales!

Use some play money, or make some out of coloured paper rectangles and cardboard circles. Don't forget to give change!

(3) Make a display

Group together your chosen foods – will you put them together by colour or by type? Count how many different kinds of food you have. Make the display look beautiful. You might, for example, set it out like a rainbow, or lay the foods out like a face, a train, or other shape. Decorate little labels to put next to each item. How much does everything cost?

(4) Go shopping

You start off as the shopkeeper and ask your toddler to visit with a favourite toy. Ask them to bring a shopping bag or basket. What would they like to buy today? Encourage them to 'try before you buy' – so they even get to taste the products, too.

50P

£1.50

10p

Swirly whirly cheesecake

This is definitely among Ella's favourite desserts of all time – it's a delicious sweet treat without any added sugar. Enjoy it when you have friends to tea.

What you need

50 g/1¾ oz **roasted hazelnuts**, finely chopped

100 g/3½ oz **Scottish oatcakes**, broken up

50 g/1¾ oz **stoned dates**

50 g/1¾ oz **unsalted butter**, melted

400 g/14 oz **cream cheese**

1 teaspoon **vanilla extract**

300 g/10½ oz **strawberries**, puréed, plus extra to serve (optional)

300 ml/½ pint **double cream**

What to do

1. Line the base of a 20 cm/8 inch loose-based cake tin with baking parchment. Put the hazelnuts and oatcakes in a food processor and blitz them for a few seconds until everything is very finely chopped and looks like breadcrumbs. Add the dates and blitz again until the mixture is soft. Add the melted butter, mix well and press the mixture into the tin with the back of a spoon. Chill this in the fridge for 15 minutes.

2. Meanwhile, make the topping. In a bowl mix together the cream cheese, vanilla extract and three-quarters of the puréed strawberries.

3. Whisk the cream until it is stiff, but still soft. Fold it gently into the cream-cheese mixture. Remove the base from the fridge and spoon over the topping.

4. Drizzle over the remaining strawberry purée in an outward spiral from the centre and then run a skewer through the spiral to get a marbled effect. Chill the cheesecake in the fridge for at least 1 hour and then serve with strawberries on the side (if using).

Can I help?

Marble-ous!

Try out your tot's artistic talents by asking him or her to have a go at making the swirly whirly marbling pattern on the top of the cheesecake.

Ella's shortcut

You can sidestep making the strawberry purée by substituting 2 x 90 g/3¼ oz pouches of Ella's Kitchen Smoothie Fruits – The Red One.

Strawberry mush up

serves 6

prep 10 minutes

This is a bit of an Eton mess, but much easier to put together. Ripe juicy strawberries, cool creamy yogurt and crunchy sweet meringue pieces create a festival of taste and texture. If you like you can drizzle extra strawberry purée on top and decorate with a few extra berries.

What you need

4 ready-made **meringue** nests (or make your own, see below)

300 g/10½ oz **strawberries**, chopped, plus a further 150 g/5½ oz fresh or frozen strawberries, puréed

200 ml/7 fl oz **Greek yogurt**

Make your meringue

If you have time, try making your own meringues. Preheat the oven to 110°C/225°F/Gas Mark ½. Whisk 3 egg whites until stiff, then whisk in 175 g/3 oz caster sugar, a teaspoon at a time. Whisk until the meringue is thick and glossy. Mix 1 teaspoon each of cornflour and of white wine vinegar with ½ teaspoon vanilla extract, and whisk this into the meringue. Spoon the mixture into 4 mounds on a parchment-lined baking sheet. Bake for 50–60 minutes.

What to do

1. Use your hands to break up the meringue nests into small pieces in a large mixing bowl. Add the chopped strawberries, reserving a few for decoration, and stir in the yogurt.

2. Add 2 tablespoons of puréed strawberries and stir through gently to make the mixture streaky.

3. Spoon the mixture into 6 glasses or bowls and decorate with a few strawberry pieces, and an extra drizzle of purée if you have it. Serve while the meringue is still crunchy.

Ella's shortcut

If you prefer, you can substitute the strawberry purée with 2 tablespoons of Ella's Kitchen Smoothie Fruits – The Red One.

Creamy coconut rice pudding with chunky mango sauce

serves 6–8 | prep 20 minutes | cook 2½ hours

A very nice lady called Cath does all the sums at Ella's Kitchen. She's also a bit of a pudding queen and has created this variation on a traditional rice pud.

What you need

25 g/1 oz **unsalted butter**

120 g/4¼ oz **pudding rice**

50 g/1¾ oz **soft light brown sugar**

400 ml/14 fl oz can **coconut milk**

300 ml/½ pint **single cream**

600 ml/1 pint **whole milk**

1 teaspoon **vanilla extract**

A pinch of **ground cinnamon**

For the mango sauce

425 g/15 oz can **sliced mangoes**

4 tablespoons **apple juice**

2 tablespoons **clear honey**

What to do

1. Preheat the oven to 150°C/300°F/Gas Mark 2 and grease an ovenproof pudding dish (30 x 20 cm/12 x 8 inches) with a little of the butter.

2. Spread the rice evenly over the base of the pudding dish. Sprinkle the sugar on top.

3. Pour the coconut milk into a separate bowl and use a balloon whisk to mix it up thoroughly. Add the cream, milk and vanilla extract and mix again.

4. Pour the coconut milk mixture over the rice and sugar, sprinkle over the cinnamon and dot the top with the remaining butter. Put the dish in the centre of the oven and bake for 2½ hours until the top is golden brown.

5. While the pudding is cooking, prepare the mango sauce. Strain the mangoes and discard the syrup. Reserve 2 of the mango slices. Purée the remaining mango in a food processor or with a hand blender until smooth. Add the apple juice and the honey and mix well. Cut the reserved mango slices into 1 cm/½ inch chunks and add them to the sauce.

6. Serve the rice pudding hot or cold with the mango sauce spooned on top.

Milk and cream

Ask your little helpers to taste a little spoon of coconut milk and then a little spoon of cream. Talk about the different tastes and textures they have and the different places that they come from.

Berry nice blueberry cream

serves 4 prep 15 minutes

Blueberries proved a definite hit with our pint-sized tasters. You can also make this fuss-free, creamy sundae for breakfast, if you prefer.

What you need

200 ml/7 fl oz **crème fraîche**

300 ml/½ pint **Greek yogurt**

Finely grated rind and juice of 1 **lemon**

300 g/10½ oz **blueberries**

1 tablespoon **clear honey**

Icing sugar, for dusting

What to do

1. Put the crème fraîche in a mixing bowl with the Greek yogurt and fold through the grated lemon rind. Divide a third of the mixture between 4 serving glasses.

2. Reserve a few blueberries for decoration. Put the remaining blueberries into a bowl with 1 tablespoon of lemon juice and the honey. Lightly mash with a potato masher, just until a few blueberries have burst, but most still remain whole. Stir the mixture well.

3. Divide half the blueberry mixture between the glasses in an even layer on top of the crème fraîche mixture. Then top with a further third of the crème fraîche mixture, the remaining blueberry mixture, and then finally the last third of the crème fraîche mixture.

4. Decorate the top of the sundae with a few of the reserved blueberries and dust with icing sugar to serve.

one for you

One for me

Smiley spiral apple tarts

Who knew apple tarts could taste this good? Little ones will love to get involved using pastry cutters and decorating the tarts with apple slices.

What you need

320 g/11¼ oz ready-made **puff pastry**

2 eating **apples** (Granny Smith or Royal Gala work best)

1 tablespoon **lemon juice**

50 g/1¾ oz **unsalted butter**, cut into 6 cubes

½ teaspoon **ground cinnamon**

25 g/1 oz **soft light brown sugar**

Roll, cut, fill

Can I help?

Tots of all ages get to play at being baker with these simple apple tarts. Making them is a brilliant activity for a play date. One friend rolls the dough, another cuts the circles and another fills the tart with pieces of apple.

What to do

1. Preheat the oven to 200°C /400°F/Gas Mark 6.

2. Roll out the puff pastry until it is 0.5 cm/¼ in thick. Using a 10 cm/4 inch pastry cutter, cut out 6 circles from the pastry and place them spaced well apart on a baking sheet.

3. Core the apples, then cut them into very thin slices and put them in a bowl with the lemon juice. Toss the apple slices well to coat them in the juice. Arrange the apple slices on top of the dough circles in a 'flower' pattern.

4. Place a cube of butter on each tart, then sprinkle the tarts with a little cinnamon (to taste) and the sugar.

5. Bake the tarts in the oven for 15–20 minutes until golden brown. Serve them warm or cold with vanilla ice cream or crème fraîche.

Wonderful watermelon ice

serves 8–10 · prep 20 minutes + freezing

A kind of kiddie granita, this is the ultimate zingy-fresh slushie. The freezing and scraping process to make the ice slush is all part of the fun.

What you need

900 g/2 lb **watermelon** flesh, cubed (about a 1.8 kg/4 lb watermelon, seeds removed)

50 g/1¾ oz **caster sugar**

Juice of 1 **lime**

Get ahead

You can make this icy pudding up to 3 days before you need it. Keep it in the freezer with the lid on the container, or tightly covered with foil. Then, when you're ready, give it a quick scrape and a mash with a fork before serving.

Save the seeds!

Don't throw away the seeds from your watermelon – dried-out seeds are brilliant for making shakers or using as 'money' in a game of shops. Rinse the discarded seeds in water and then lay them out on kitchen paper in a warm place for 7–10 days. The seeds are completely dry when they snap rather than bend between your fingers.

What to do

1. Put all the ingredients in a food processor and whiz until smooth (you can put everything in a bowl and use a hand blender if you don't have a food processor).

2. Pour the mixture into a shallow freezer container, put the lid on and freeze the mixture for 1 hour.

3. Remove the mixture from the freezer and stir it well, mashing any frozen parts with the back of a fork.

4. Replace the lid and freeze the mixture for a further 2 hours until firm.

5. Using a fork, scrape the frozen mixture vigorously to form icy flakes. Serve in plastic cups or small glasses.

Colour me in

Zingy pineapple with basil + lime

These ingredients sound quite grown up, but we've found that older toddlers are interested to find out about the zesty tastes and textures – and then love them when they tuck in.

What you need

Finely grated rind and juice of 1 **lime**

50 g/1¾ oz **soft dark brown sugar**

1 tablespoon finely chopped **basil** leaves

1 whole **pineapple**, peeled, cored and cut into 'soldier'-like slices

What to do

1. Place the lime rind and juice in a bowl and stir in the sugar and basil. Leave the mixture to marinate for 5 minutes until the sugar has dissolved to form a syrup.

2. Arrange the pineapple 'soldiers' on a large serving plate and drizzle over some of the lime and basil syrup. Put any remaining syrup in a little bowl for extra dunking. Serve immediately.

Smell-a-thon

Crushing the basil releases its delicious smell – talk to your toddler about it and what it might remind you of. Summertime? Pizza? And what about the smell of the lime? How is that different from the pineapple?

Make it mango

As an alternative you can substitute the pineapple with 2 fresh mangoes, peeled and sliced for a different kind of tropical flavour.

Dip me in

Fabulous fruit compote

You can enjoy this versatile fruit compote for breakfast served with yogurt and granola, as a hot or cold snack, or for a dinner-time pud served with ice cream or custard.

What you need

2 eating **apples**, peeled, cored and diced

2 **conference pears**, peeled, cored and diced

350 g/12 oz **plums**, stoned and diced

75 g/2½ oz **dried prunes**, roughly chopped

50 g/1¾ oz **sultanas**

Finely grated rind and juice of 1 **orange**

½ teaspoon **mixed spice**

What to do

1. Place all the ingredients in a medium saucepan, cover with a lid and cook gently for 20 minutes, stirring occasionally, until the fruit has softened but there is still some texture.

2. Remove the pan from the heat. Serve the compote warm or cold.

Hello...

Scrummy treats

Hello!
How many bananas
can you spot in
this chapter?
Love, Ella x

Teeny weeny fruit muffins

The fruit purée makes these muffins *reeeally* moist. The muffins are easy peasy to make, and bake in 20 minutes, so provide a perfect afternoon cooking activity when a friend comes to play. Mmmm ... warm muffins to keep them going until tea. Perfect.

What you need

75 g/2½ oz **unsalted butter**, softened

50 g/1¾ oz **caster sugar**

1 **egg**

75 g/2½ oz **wholemeal flour**

1 teaspoon **baking powder**

125 g/4½ oz **strawberries** or **raspberries**, puréed (reserve a few whole berries)

50 g/1¾ oz **raisins**

50 g/1¾ oz finely **chopped walnuts** (optional)

Porridge oats, to sprinkle

What to do

1. Preheat the oven to 180°C/350°F/Gas Mark 4. Line a mini muffin tin with paper cake cases.

2. Cream together the butter and sugar in a large bowl until light and fluffy. Add the egg and stir in well to combine. Sift in the flour and baking powder and stir again. Finally, stir in the puréed strawberry or raspberry and the raisins, then the walnuts (if using).

3. Divide the mixture between the cake cases, filling each about three-quarters full so that the muffins have room to rise. Sprinkle a few porridge oats over each muffin.

4. Bake for 20 minutes until the muffins are firm to the touch and golden brown on top.

5. Cool them on a wire rack before serving. They will keep in an airtight container for up to 3 days.

Bake away!

Can I help?

This is a baking extravaganza for tiny helpers. Little ones can get stuck in with the creaming, the egg-cracking, the sifting, the stirring and the sprinkling – so much to do, so much messy fun to be had.

Ella's shortcut

To save time, you can replace the puréed strawberries or raspberries with 1 x 90 g/3 oz pouch of Ella's Kitchen Smoothie Fruits – The Red One.

Rise 'n' shine banana bread

makes **10** slices · prep **10** minutes · cook **1¼** hours

This simple banana bread is deliciously moist and ideal for a late breakfast, as a snack for a trip to the park, or with a cup of juice mid-afternoon.

What you need

310 g/11 oz ripe **bananas**, mashed

2 tablespoons **agave syrup**

3 **eggs**

250 g/9 oz **self-raising flour**

1 teaspoon **baking powder**

1 teaspoon **bicarbonate of soda**

25 g/1 oz **butter**, cubed

What to do

1. Preheat the oven to 160°C/315°F/Gas Mark 2–3. Lightly oil a 900 g/2 lb loaf tin.

2. Put the mashed banana, agave syrup and eggs in a bowl and use a wooden spoon to beat the ingredients together until well combined.

3. In a separate large bowl, sift together the flour, baking powder and bicarbonate of soda, then use your fingertips to rub in the butter until the mixture resembles fine breadcrumbs.

4. Tip the egg and banana mixture into the dry ingredients and mix them together until well combined. Spoon the mixture into the prepared loaf tin and level the top. Bake the banana bread for 1 hour to 1 hour and 15 minutes until well risen and golden, and hollow-sounding when you tap the base.

5. Cool the loaf in the tin, then turn it out and cut into slices to serve.

Choccie chocolate munchies

makes **16** squares

prep **25** minutes + chilling

This is a fave with all little cookie monsters and there's no baking required, which means that they can get involved in every stage of the making ... as well as the eating!

What you need

200 g/7 oz **digestive biscuits**

100 g/3½ oz **unsalted butter**, plus extra for greasing

3 tablespoons **golden syrup**

2 tablespoons **cocoa powder**

50 g/1¾ oz **raisins**

100 g/3½ oz **dark chocolate**, broken into pieces

Munchie making

Can I help?

Get your little ones inolved in the biscuit bashing in this recipe. Ask for help breaking up, melting and pouring over the chocolate, too.

What to do

1. Butter an 18 cm/7 inch sandwich tin. Either seal the biscuits inside a strong polythene bag or place them in a large plastic bowl. Pound the biscuits with a rolling pin to bash them up into uneven crumbs.

2. Melt the butter and golden syrup in a saucepan. Stir in the cocoa powder and raisins, then thoroughly stir in the biscuit crumbs. Spoon the mixture into the prepared tin and press down firmly all over. Put the mixture in the fridge to chill for 10 minutes.

3. Meanwhile, melt the chocolate pieces in a heatproof bowl over a pan of simmering water (or melt the chocolate in a microwave on medium for 2–3 minutes). Remove the biscuit mixture from the fridge and spread the melted chocolate over it. Return it to the fridge to chill for a further 30 minutes until firm and set.

4. Remove the firm munchie mixture from the tin, put it on a chopping board and cut it into 16 squares. You can store the munchies in an airtight container in the fridge for up to a week.

How high can I go?

Nicely spicy veggie crisps

serves 4 · prep 20 minutes · cook 20 minutes

Kids love crunchy snacks and our healthy alternative to standard potato crisps has extra veggie goodness without losing any of the munchiness.

What you need

2 **parsnips**

1 **sweet potato**

1 raw **beetroot**

2 tablespoons **olive oil**

¼ teaspoon **mild chilli powder**

What to do

1. Preheat the oven to 220°C/425°F/Gas Mark 7.

2. Using a potato peeler or mandoline (take care!), slice the vegetables on the diagonal very thinly to create wafer-thin crisps, approximately 2 mm/$^1/_{16}$ inch thick. Spread out the vegetable slices on kitchen paper to draw out any excess moisture.

3. Place the parsnips and sweet potato slices into a bowl with 1 tablespoon of the olive oil and the chilli powder and toss to lightly coat, then spread them out on a baking sheet. Place the beetroot slices into a bowl with the remaining oil and toss well. Spread out the beetroot on another baking sheet.

4. Roast all the vegetables in the centre of the preheated oven for 20 minutes, turning them halfway through cooking if necessary, until they are crisp.

5. Remove the baking sheets from the oven and spread out the vegetable crisps on paper towels to cool slightly before serving. Eat immediately.

5

Five ways with popcorn

Popcorn is a great weekend treat that all the family can enjoy – ideally in front of a favourite film.

serves 4 · prep 5 minutes · cook 5 minutes

Basic popcorn recipe

75 g/2½ oz **popping corn**

Put the popping corn in a very large saucepan and place it over a high heat covered with a lid.

Holding the lid, cook the popcorn for about 3–5 minutes until it begins to pop. It will pop repeatedly and then finally stop popping altogether. Shake the pan continuously throughout the process to keep it moving.

Turn off the heat and remove the lid from the pan to allow the popcorn to cool a little before adding the flavouring of your choice.

Cheesy popcorn

1 quantity basic **popcorn** (above)

75 g/2½ oz **Parmesan cheese**, grated

½ teaspoon **mild chilli powder** (optional)

Scatter the Parmesan in batches over the freshly cooked, warm popcorn, shaking the pan gently and stirring through each batch of cheese before adding the next. Keep going until all the popcorn is lightly covered and the cheese has melted a little.

Scatter over ½ teaspoon mild chilli powder (if using) before serving.

Bacon-flavoured popcorn

1 quantity basic **popcorn** (opposite)

50 g/1¾ oz **unsalted butter**

125 g/4½ oz **unsmoked back bacon**, finely shredded

Heat the butter in a large frying pan and gently cook the bacon for 2–3 minutes until just beginning to crisp.

Once the popcorn has cooked, pour in the butter and bacon mixture and toss with the popcorn until lightly covered. Serve warm.

Caramel popcorn

1 quantity basic **popcorn** (opposite)

50 g/1¾ oz **unsalted butter**

2 tablespoons **light muscovado sugar**

2 tablespoons **double cream**

Heat the butter in a small saucepan, then add the sugar and stir well for about 2 minutes until the sugar dissolves.

Remove the pan from the heat and add the cream, stirring well until a caramel has formed. Pour this over the freshly cooked popcorn and gently toss to lightly coat.

Peanut butter popcorn

1 quantity basic **popcorn** (opposite)

25 g/1 oz **unsalted butter**

2 tablespoons **soft brown sugar**

3 tablespoons **smooth peanut butter**

Heat the butter in a large saucepan, then add the sugar and stir well for about 2 minutes until the sugar dissolves. Stir in the peanut butter.

Add the cooked popcorn to the pan with the peanut butter mixture, in batches, and gently toss to lightly coat.

Cinnamon popcorn

1 quantity basic **popcorn** (opposite)

50 g/1¾ oz **unsalted butter**

2 tablespoons **demerara sugar**

½ teaspoon **ground cinnamon**

Heat the butter in a small saucepan, then add the sugar and cinnamon and stir well for about 2 minutes until the sugar dissolves.

Pour the cinnamon mixture over the freshly made popcorn and gently toss to lightly coat.

Mix + match crumbly cookies

makes 20–24 | prep 30 minutes + chilling | cook 10 minutes

This cookie-dough combination was made to inspire budding designers. From splats to plaits and from rocks to rolls, let imaginations go wild and little fingers get messy!

What you need

175 g/6 oz **unsalted butter**

150 g/5½ oz **caster sugar**

1 teaspoon **vanilla extract**

1 **egg**

200 g/7 oz **plain flour**

1 teaspoon **baking powder**

2 tablespoons **cocoa powder**

1 tablespoon finely grated **orange** rind

Cookie art

Rolling, squishing and cutting the cookie dough are cooking activities simply made for tiny hands. Get the kids involved all the way through with this one.

What to do

1) Preheat the oven to 180°C/350°F/Gas Mark 4.

2) In a medium bowl, cream together the butter, sugar and vanilla extract until smooth. Beat in the egg. In a separate bowl, combine the flour and baking powder, then stir the dry ingredients into the butter and sugar mixture. Combine until you have a soft dough.

3) Divide the dough in half. Add the cocoa powder to one half, kneading the dough until it is completely chocolatey. Add the orange rind to the remaining dough, kneading it through as before.

4) Place each piece of dough onto a well-floured surface and, using your hands, create cylindrical sausage-shapes of about 30 cm/ 12 inches long from each type of dough. Lay 1 chocolate and 1 orange dough cylinder side by side and, beginning at one end, turn the cylinders to create a spiral. Repeat for all the dough cylinders.

5) Place your combined dough pieces onto a baking sheet and freeze for 10 minutes to firm up. When chilled, flatten each wheel with a rolling pin, then use cookie cutters to cut 2-tone shapes from the dough.

6) Place the cookies, spaced well apart, onto a large baking sheet lined with baking parchment and bake for 8–10 minutes until cooked through. Cool on a wire rack.

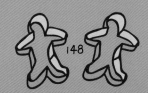

Awesome orange and ginger cake

makes
8
squares

prep
20
minutes

cook
30-35
minutes

This cake is a sweet and scrummy introduction to ginger – have fun helping your little ones discover new tastes for their developing taste buds.

What you need

75 g/2½ oz **unsalted butter**

150 g/5½ oz **golden syrup** or **black treacle**

225 g/8 oz **self-raising flour**

2 teaspoons **ground ginger**

1 teaspoon **ground cinnamon**

225 g/8 oz coarse cut **orange marmalade**

1 **egg**, beaten

1 tablespoon freshly squeezed **orange juice**

What to do

1. Preheat the oven to 180°C/350°F/Gas Mark 4. Grease a 20 cm/8 inch square cake tin and line the base with baking parchment.

2. Melt the butter and syrup in a saucepan over a low heat, stirring well to combine. Remove the mixture from the heat and set aside.

3. Sift the flour, ginger and cinnamon into a bowl, then slowly pour the syrup mixture into the flour mixture and stir to combine. Add the marmalade, egg, orange juice and 1 tablespoon of hot water and combine to make a soft mixture. Add a further 1–2 tablespoons of hot water if it is too stiff.

4. Pour the mixture into the cake tin and spread evenly. Bake the cake for 30–35 minutes until golden and firm to the touch.

5. Allow the cake to cool for 15 minutes in the tin before carefully removing it to a wire rack. Serve it warm with a scoop of vanilla ice cream, or cold with a glass of freshly squeezed orange juice.

I might be a bit too hot for your pocket!

Pizza pocket bites

makes **8** | prep **20** minutes | cook **25** minutes
+ proving

These are no ordinary bread rolls – they're bite-sized and have pizza flavours buried in the centre to tantalise the taste buds. Eat them on their own or as an accompaniment to pasta dishes. You can leave out the pepperoni for a veggie alternative.

What you need

2 x 145 g/5¼ oz packets **pizza-base mix**

2 tablespoons finely chopped **oregano**

1 tablespoon **olive oil**

¼ each small **red**, **yellow** and **green pepper**, roughly sliced

50 g/1¾ oz **pepperoni**, roughly chopped

100 g/3½ oz **Cheddar cheese**, grated

What to do

1. Preheat the oven to 220°C/425°F/Gas Mark 7.

2. Put the pizza base dough in a bowl with the oregano, add the required amount of warm water according to the packet instructions and mix thoroughly to form a smooth dough.

3. Turn out the dough onto a lightly floured surface and knead it until it is smooth.

4. Heat the oil in a heavy-based frying pan and cook the peppers over a moderate heat for 4–5 minutes until soft, then add the pepperoni and cook for a further 1 minute.

5. Divide the dough into 8 pieces and make a well in the centre of each. Divide the peppers and pepperoni between the dough pieces and very roughly knead them into the dough, then shape the dough pieces into rough balls and place them on a baking sheet. Cover the balls with a damp cloth and leave them to prove for 30 minutes, or until they have roughly doubled in size.

6. Sprinkle the balls with the Cheddar and bake them for 20 minutes until they are golden and cooked through – when they're cooked, the base of each pizza bite should sound hollow when you tap it. Serve the pizza bites while they are still warm.

Kneading time

Can I help?

Your toddler can help you to knead the veggies into the dough pieces and roll them into balls – brilliant foody play that helps to get the job done!

153

Flour dough fun

Our special cloud dough is so much fun – and best of all it's super-easy to make. It's also messy, so give everyone an apron and cover the table before you get started.

① Mix it up

In a bowl mix together 8 cups of cornflour and 1–2 cups of vegetable oil. Work it all together to combine. Little fingers get stuck in straightaway – getting messy is all part of the fun.

② Add the sparkle

Add in a few sprinkles of glitter and mix them through. Now it's like fairy dust! The dough should hold together when moulded gently, but crumble away if you apply pressure.

3

Watch the magic

When it's all fully mixed together, it's time to play. Put the cloud dough into a large tray, then mould it into shapes – a bit like building lots of sparkly sandcastles. When you're ready, knock them down and build some more!

Magic goop

When you've had enough of cloud dough, try magic goop instead. In a big bowl mix together 500 g/1 lb 2 oz cornflour and 2 cups of water. Add food colouring – the brighter the better, but be careful, as it may stain your clothes. Then, watch! At first the goop feels quite firm, but suddenly it will stream through little fingers like magic. Make your goop sparkle by adding some twinkly glitter; or make it smell delicious with a drop or two of peppermint essence.

Cheesy straw dippers

serves 4 | prep 20 minutes | cook 15 minutes

We think these are the flakiest, cheesiest, most perfect cheese straws we've ever tasted. They taste even better when they're dunked in our cheesy pesto dip.

What you need

50 g/1¾ oz **unsalted butter**, softened

250 g/9 oz **Cheddar cheese**, grated

125 g/4½ oz **wholemeal flour**

1 **egg**, lightly beaten

2 tablespoons **sesame seeds**

¼ teaspoon **mild chilli powder** or **paprika**

For the pesto dip

2 tablespoons **pesto** or our **Green Pasta Sauce** (see page 96)

50 g/1¾ oz **cream cheese**

2 tablespoons **whole milk**

What to do

1. Preheat the oven to 200°C/400°F/Gas Mark 6.

2. In a food processor cream the butter and Cheddar. Stir in the flour and form the mixture into a soft dough.

3. On a lightly floured surface roll out the dough until it is 1.5 cm/⅝ inch thick. Brush the flattened dough with the beaten egg, then cut it into 5 cm/2 inch strips. Sprinkle the strips with the sesame seeds and the chilli powder or paprika.

4. Put the strips on a lightly greased baking sheet and bake them for 10–15 minutes until crisp.

5. Meanwhile, make the pesto dip by mixing the pesto or Green Pasta Sauce with the cream cheese and the milk until fully combined. Put the dip in a small dipping bowl and serve with the warm cheese straws.

Rollin' rollin' rollin'

Can I help?

Lightly flour your surface, put down your ball of cheesy dough and let your little helper roll away. Once the dough is flat, he or she can brush over the egg glaze, too.

Carroty cakes

Carrots make a wonderfully moist cake. These little treats are especially good because the decorations are made from real carrot shavings.

What you need

200 g/7 oz **carrots**

175 g/6 oz **soft brown sugar**

200 g/7 oz **self-raising flour**

1 teaspoon **bicarbonate of soda**

2 teaspoons **ground cinnamon**

Finely grated rind of 1 **orange**

2 **eggs**, beaten

150 ml/¼ pint **sunflower oil**

For the topping

50 g/1¾ oz **unsalted butter**, softened

75 g/2½ oz **icing sugar**

120 g/4¼ oz **cream cheese**

Carrot shavings, to decorate (optional)

What to do

1. Preheat the oven to 180°C/350°F/Gas Mark 4. Grease an 18 cm/7 inch square cake tin.

2. Grate the carrots finely into a large mixing bowl. Sift the sugar, flour, bicarbonate of soda and cinnamon on top of the carrot, then add the orange rind and mix everything together. Add the eggs and the oil to the mixture. Mix everything together well.

3. Spoon the mixture into the cake tin and level the top. Bake for 30 minutes or until the cake is cooked through – test it by piercing it with a metal skewer. It should come out clean. Remove the cake from the oven and leave it to cool in the tin placed on a wire rack.

4. Meanwhile, make the topping. Mix the butter and icing sugar together, then stir in the cream cheese until smooth.

5. When the cake is cool, carefully turn it out onto a board. Spread the topping evenly over the cake and cut the cake into 16 squares. Decorate each square with a shaving of fresh carrot, if you wish.

Everyone loves a lazy weekend breakfast –
especially if it occasionally turns into lunch!
Here are some tasty ideas for leisurely breakfasts
that little ones can get involved in making themselves –
with a little bit of supervision from the grown-ups.

Very berry smoothie

serves
4

prep
5
minutes

Full of fruity goodness and great for slurping, this smoothie is always a hit.

75 g/2½ oz **vanilla yogurt**
175 g/6 oz **frozen berries** or **fresh fruit** (mango, pineapple, raspberries, or whatever is in season)
1 ripe **banana**
150 ml/¼ pint **fruit juice** (any flavour)

Place all the ingredients into a food processor and whiz until smooth. Pour into 4 glasses and serve immediately.

What colour?

Before you whiz up the fruit, have a go at guessing what colour the smoothie is going to be. Talk about the colours of the individual fruits and then older toddlers can try to predict the result.

Purple pancakes

Who said pancakes have to be yellow? Squished blueberries added to the batter make pancakes that are purple – a special surprise for the weekend.

150 g/5½ oz **self-raising flour**

1 **egg**

150 ml/¼ pint **whole milk**

50 g/1¾ oz **blueberries**

Unsalted butter, for frying

Maple syrup, to serve (optional)

Fresh fruit, to serve (optional)

Sift the flour into a small mixing bowl and make a well in the centre.

Break the egg into a jug, add the milk, and mix well. Pour the mixture into the well and, using a balloon whisk, draw the flour into the liquid gradually and mix it all together until combined to a smooth batter.

Place the blueberries in a small bowl and, using a hand blender, whiz until almost smooth and very purple!

Pour the purple purée into the pancake batter and mix well.

Wipe the base of a large heavy-based frying pan with a little butter, and heat. Pour large spoonfuls of the batter, spaced well apart, into the the pan and cook the pancakes for about 1 minute, then flip them over using a fish slice and cook for 30 seconds to 1 minute more on the other side until golden brown on both sides.

Remove the pancakes from the pan and keep them warm. Repeat the process until all the batter is used up. Serve the pancakes warm with a little maple syrup and fresh fruit (if using).

Can I help?

Scale school

Measuring out the blueberries is a good introduction to using scales for little ones – and less messy than measuring out flour or sugar!

Holey moley pancakes

makes 12 · prep 10 minutes · cook 6 minutes

This is a variation on pikelets, courtesy of Kim who runs our Making Friends team here at Ella's Kitchen. She loves to make them with her nieces and nephews when they come to stay. The little holes are the secret to a great pancake taste experience.

125 g/4½ oz **plain flour**	
½ teaspoon **baking soda**	
½ teaspoon **cream of tartar**	
1 **egg**	
1 tablespoon **sugar**	
25 g/1 oz **unsalted butter**, melted, plus extra for frying	
150 ml/¼ pint **whole milk**	
Fresh fruit, to serve (optional)	

Mix the flour with the baking powder and cream of tartar. In a separate bowl, cream the egg and sugar, then stir in the melted butter. Then, alternately add small amounts of the flour mixture and the milk to the egg mixture until everything is combined to a thick batter.

Wipe the base of a large heavy-based frying pan with a little butter, and heat. Spoon in individual tablespoons of the batter to form small pancakes. Cook for about 1 minute until the bubbles have burst, then flip the pancakes over using a fish slice and cook for 30 seconds more until golden brown on both sides.

Remove the pancakes from the pan and keep them warm. Repeat the process until all the batter is used up. Serve the pancakes warm with fresh fruit (if using).

Strawberry, banana + mango porridge

serves **4** | prep **10** minutes | cook **10** minutes

This deliciously fruity porridge is just about the perfect start to the day – a warming breakfast that the whole family will want to try!

1 large **banana**, roughly chopped

125 g/4½ oz **strawberries**, hulled and roughly chopped

½ **mango**, roughly chopped

1½ tablespoons **clear honey**

½ teaspoon **ground cinnamon**

600 ml/1 pint **whole milk**

150 g/5½ oz **porridge oats**

Place the fruit in a saucepan with the honey, the cinnamon and 2 tablespoons of water. Bring to the boil, stir gently to combine, and over a medium heat cook for 3–4 minutes until the fruit is soft and a toffee-like sauce has formed.

In a separate pan, bring the milk to the boil, stirring occasionally, then remove it from the heat and add the porridge oats. Stir well, then return the pan to a low heat, stirring continuously for 5–6 minutes until the porridge has thickened.

Stir half the fruit mixture through the porridge and mix well, then ladle the fruity porridge into warmed serving bowls and spoon over the remaining fruit.

Slowly, slowly stirring

Can I help?

Older children can help you stir the porridge slowly – but keep a very attentive eye on them the whole time. Talk about how the mixture changes from runny to thick.

5 ways

Five ways with eggs

Lazy weekend breakfasts are made for sharing. We love that the humble egg lets us rustle up so many tastes and textures.

Scrambled egg + avocado

serves 2–4 | prep 5 minutes | cook 5 minutes

4 **eggs**, beaten

Unsalted butter, for frying

4 tablespoons **crème fraîche**

1 small **avocado**, roughly chopped

¼ teaspoon **paprika**

Freshly ground **black pepper**

Place the eggs in a small heavy-based saucepan with the butter and cook them over a low heat, stirring continuously until the eggs begin to cook.

Remove the eggs from the heat, season with a little pepper, then add the crème fraîche. Return the mixture to the heat and cook, stirring continuously, until the egg is cooked through, but the mixture is still soft.

Remove the eggs from the heat, stir in the avocado and paprika and serve with wholemeal toast fingers.

Lemon soufflé cloud omelette

serves 2 | prep 5 minutes | cook 4 minutes

3 **eggs**, separated

Finely grated rind and juice of 1 **lemon**

1 tablespoon **caster sugar**

Unsalted butter, for frying

1 teaspoon **icing sugar**

Whisk the egg whites until stiff. In a separate bowl mix together the egg yolks, the lemon juice and rind and the sugar.

Heat the butter in a medium-sized frying pan. Fold the egg whites and yolk mixture together, then pour it all into the pan.

Cook the omelette over a gentle heat for 2–3 minutes on one side, then flip it over and cook the other side for about 30 seconds until both sides are just golden.

Turn the omelette out of the pan onto a warmed serving plate and sprinkle with icing sugar.

Red cheesy scramble

Unsalted butter, for frying

4 eggs

4 tablespoons whole milk

75 g/2½ oz red Leicester cheese, grated

Heat the butter in a small heavy-based saucepan over a low heat.

Beat the eggs, milk and red Leicester with a wooden spoon, then pour into the pan.

Stir continuously over the heat for 3–4 minutes until the eggs are softly scrambled and cooked through, and the cheese has melted.

Serve on a slice of toasted wholemeal soda bread if liked.

Posh ham + eggs

4 eggs

2 muffins, halved and toasted

4 thick slices good-quality ham

4 tablespoons hollandaise sauce

To poach the eggs, bring a small saucepan of lightly salted water to the boil. Stir the water briskly to create a whirlpool and then crack the eggs into it, 1 or 2 at a time, and cook for 2–3 minutes. Remove the eggs from the pan using a slotted spoon and keep warm.

Lightly toast the muffins and place each toasted half on a warmed serving plate. Top with a slice of ham and a poached egg. Spoon 1 tablespoon of hollandaise sauce over each egg to serve.

Cinnamon eggy bread

2 eggs, beaten

100 ml/3½ fl oz whole milk

1 teaspoon ground cinnamon

4 slices brioche

Unsalted butter, for frying

4 teaspoons demerara sugar

Place the eggs in a small bowl with the milk and ½ teaspoon of the cinnamon and beat together. Dip the brioche slices into the milk mixture, allowing it to soak in a little. Melt the butter in a large heavy-based frying pan, then cook the eggy bread over a high heat for 1–2 minutes on each side until lightly golden. Mix the demerara sugar with the remaining cinnamon and sprinkle over the eggy bread.

For a bit of a special treat, why not have a day dedicated to chocolate! Have fun experimenting with different combinations of fruit and chocolate, or have a go at making the best chocolate cake ever. There's nothing quite like the gooey, chocolatey mess that happens when you tuck in!

Warm chocolate pots

serves **6** | prep **5** minutes | cook **5** minutes

This is a yummy cross between chocolate mousse and warm chocolate pot and we dare anyone not to like it! It's ideal for chocolate moustaches.

300 g/10½ oz **dark chocolate**, broken up
500 g/1 lb 2 oz **fromage frais**
1 teaspoon **vanilla extract**
cocoa powder, for dusting (optional)

Melt the chocolate in a bowl over a pan of gently simmering water. When the chocolate has melted, remove the pan from the heat.

Take the bowl off the pan and add the fromage frais and vanilla extract, quickly stirring it all together until the ingredients are fully combined.

Divide the chocolate fromage frais between 6 little pots, cups or glasses. Dust with cocoa powder (if using) and serve immediately.

Fruity fun choccie dippers

serves **4** | prep **5** minutes | cook **10** minutes

Delicious pieces of fruit dunked in 3 kinds of runny chocolate – lip-smackingly good!

200 g/7 oz **milk chocolate**, broken up
200 g/7 oz **white chocolate**, broken up
200 g/7 oz **dark chocolate**, broken up
Slices of **apple**, **pear**, **melon** and **pineapple**, halved **grapes** and whole **strawberries**, for dunking

Put the pieces of milk, white and dark chocolate into 3 separate bowls.

In turn, place each bowl over a pan of gently simmering water and melt the 3 types of chocolate until each becomes smooth, glossy and runny.

Transfer each type of chocolate into its own serving dish and serve immediately with bowls of the fruit on the side for dunking.

Best-ever chocolate cake

Whether it be for a birthday or other celebration, or a simple afternoon tea, every family needs a best-ever chocolate cake recipe. Listen for the chorus of 'More, please!'

150 g/5½ oz **plain flour**

50 g/1¾ oz good-quality **cocoa powder**

1 heaped teaspoon **baking powder**

175 g/6 oz **unsalted butter**, softened

150 g/5½ oz **light muscovado sugar**

3 **eggs**, beaten

250 ml/9 fl oz **soured cream**

1 tsp **vanilla essence**

For the icing

100 g/3½ oz **plain chocolate**, broken up

150 g/5½ oz **unsalted butter**, softened

125 g/4½ oz **cream cheese**

175 g/6 oz **icing sugar**, sifted

50 g/1¾ oz **milk**, **dark** and **white chocolate**, grated, to decorate

Preheat the oven to 180°C/350°F/Gas Mark 4. Grease a 20 cm/8 inch springform cake tin and line it with baking parchment.

Sift the flour, cocoa powder and baking powder into a bowl. In a separate bowl, cream together the butter and muscovado sugar until light and fluffy. A little at a time, add the beaten eggs with a spoonful of the flour mixture to the butter mixture, stirring continuously.

Add in the remaining flour mixture along with the soured cream and vanilla essence and fold everything together using a metal spoon. Spoon the cake batter into the prepared tin and bake for 40–50 minutes until the cake has risen and is firm to the touch. The cake is ready when a skewer inserted into the centre comes out clean. Cool the cake in the tin for 20 minutes, then turn it out onto a wire rack to cool completely.

Meanwhile make the icing. Melt the chocolate in a bowl set over a pan of gently simmering water. Once it has melted, set it aside to cool. In a separate bowl beat the butter and cream cheese with a wooden spoon until combined. Beat in the icing sugar, then the cooled chocolate, taking care not to overbeat.

Cut the cooked cake in half horizontally and use a third of the icing to sandwich the two pieces together. Transfer the cake to a serving board or plate and cover the top and sides with the remaining icing. Decorate with the grated chocolate.

The smell of homemade pizza baking in the oven is utterly delicious. Transforming your kitchen into a pizza café means there's plenty for everyone to do – from creating the menus and taking the orders to preparing the pizza dough and arranging the toppings. Have fun!

Potato pizza

100 g/3½ oz **plain flour**

¼ teaspoon **fast-action dried yeast**

2 teaspoons **sugar**

75 g/2½ oz mashed **potato**

1 **egg**, beaten

5 tablespoons **pizza sauce** or **Clever Tomato Sauce** (see page 32)

6 **sunblush tomatoes**

75 g/2½ oz **mozzarella cheese**, grated

Basil leaves, to serve

In a small bowl, combine the flour, yeast and sugar. Add the mashed potato and mix. The dough should look clumpy. Add 3 tablespoons of water and then the egg and stir with a spatula until the mixture forms a loose dough.

Knead the dough on a lightly floured surface until it becomes smooth. Put it in a bowl, cover the bowl with a damp tea towel and set the dough aside to prove for 30 minutes in a warm place.

Preheat the oven to 200°C/400°F/Gas Mark 6.

Knead the dough again on a lightly floured surface and roll it out to a circle measuring about 20 cm/8 inches in diameter and place this on a large baking sheet. Lightly cover the dough with a tea towel and allow it to rest for a further 15 minutes. After this time, spread the dough with the pizza sauce or Clever Tomato Sauce, tomatoes and mozzarella.

Bake the pizza in the preheated oven for 20 minutes until the mozzarella is bubbling and golden. Scatter the pizza with basil leaves and serve cut into wedges. (Try some of the other topping suggestions on page 179, too.)

Roaring rocket pizza

serves **4** · prep **5** minutes · cook **8–10** minutes

This is the quickest pizza ever, and the rocket adds some greens. Children love the stringiness of the mozzarella.

4 small round **wholemeal pitta breads**

4 tablespoons **concentrated tomato purée** or **Clever Tomato Sauce** (see page 32)

125 g/4½ oz **mozzarella cheese**, cut into slices (or 4 handfuls of ready-grated mozzarella)

2 handfuls of **rocket** leaves

Preheat the oven to 220°C/425°F/Gas Mark 7.

Place the pitta breads on a baking sheet and spread each pitta evenly with the tomato purée or Clever Tomato Sauce, then cover each with mozzarella.

Bake the pizzas in the middle of the oven for 8–10 minutes, or until the cheese is melted and has turned golden brown.

Allow the cooked pizzas to cool for a few minutes, then sprinkle with rocket leaves and serve immediately.

Pesto pizza?

You can vary the toppings, and also the sauce. Instead of the purée or Clever Tomato Sauce, try spreading each pitta bread with 2 teaspoons of tomato pesto from a jar.

DIY pizza pie

Can I help?

Spreading over luscious helpings of tomato purée with a plastic knife, or with a butter knife that has a rounded end, is a great way for children to get involved. They can sprinkle over their own toppings, too.

Colour me in

Scone pizza

Pizzas don't have to be round. Use a cookie cutter to create your favourite shape. Choose your toppings. Adding herbs to the scone mixture in these pizzas makes for extra tastiness.

500 g/1 lb 2 oz **self-raising flour**

250 g/9 oz **ricotta cheese**

1 **egg**

3 tablespoons finely chopped mixed **fresh herbs** (such as basil, parsley and oregano)

4 **sun-dried tomatoes**, drained and roughly chopped

250 ml/9 fl oz **whole milk**

4 tablespoons **sun-dried tomato purée** or **Clever Tomato Sauce** (see page 32)

75 g/2½ oz **black olives**, pitted and roughly chopped

75 g/2½ oz **mozzarella cheese**, finely chopped

Freshly ground **black pepper**, to taste

Preheat the oven to 200°C/400°F/ Gas Mark 6.

Sift the flour into a food processor fitted with the plastic blade and season with a little freshly ground black pepper.

In a bowl, beat the ricotta, egg, herbs, tomatoes and milk together well. Add this cheese mixture to the flour in the food processor and beat to make a soft dough.

Turn out the dough onto a lightly floured surface. Roll it out to form a rough 23 cm/ 9 inch circle. (Cut your dough shapes now if you wish.) Place the dough circle or shapes on a baking sheet.

Spread the dough with the sun-dried tomato purée or Clever Tomato Sauce, scatter with the olives and sprinkle over the chopped mozzarella.

Bake for 25 minutes until the cheese is golden and bubbling.

Create your own

Can I help?

Mini chefs will love to roll out the dough and then use their favourite shape cutters to make their own personalised pizzas. They can help with the cheese sprinkling, too.

Toppings to try

- Peppers
- Ham
- Mushrooms
- Grated courgette
- Fresh pineapple
- Cooked sliced aubergine
- Sun-dried tomatoes
- Canned tuna
- Cooked prawns
- Cooked chicken (try some teriyaki chicken)
- Sweetcorn
- Olives
- Cooked egg
- Cooked sausage
- Chocolate + banana

Cooking outdoors

The sight, sound and smell of food sizzling on the BBQ is one of summer's great delights. Children will love to be involved in the grilling process, with careful supervision. Little hands also make light work of kebab preparations, wrapping food in foil parcels and mixing salads and sauces.

Inside-out burgers

makes **8** · prep **15** minutes · cook **5** minutes

500 g/1 lb 2 oz **lean minced beef**

3 tablespoons finely chopped **flat-leaf parsley**

1 tablespoon **wholegrain mustard**

125 g/4½ oz **Gruyère cheese**, cut into 8 small equal slices

8 small **wholemeal burger buns**, to serve

Rocket leaves and **tomato** slices, to serve

Freshly ground **black pepper**

Place the minced beef in a bowl, add the parsley and mustard, season well with plenty of freshly ground black pepper, and mix well with a fork.

Divide the mixture into 8 equal pieces. Break each piece in half and shape each half into a thin patty. Top one of the patties with a slice of Gruyère (the cheese should sit within the patty with at least a 1 cm/½ inch border around it – shape the meat into a larger patty, if necessary). Place the other patty over the top and press down around the edges to secure the cheese inside. Prepare the rest of the burgers in the same way.

Cook the burgers on a wire rack over the hot coals for 4–5 minutes on each side until coloured and cooked through.

Serve the burgers in wholemeal buns with rocket leaves and tomato slices.

Sticky sausages

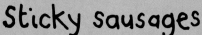

serves 4–6 | prep 5 minutes | cook 10–12 minutes

12 good-quality **chipolata sausages**

1 tablespoon **olive oil**

For the glaze

3 tablespoons **clear honey**

2 tablespoons **wholegrain mustard**

2 tablespoons finely chopped **flat-leaf parsley**

Freshly ground **black pepper**

Place the sausages on a wire rack over the hot coals and cook them for 10–12 minutes, turning them until they are browned all over and cooked through. Remove the sausages from the heat and cut each sausage in half.

Place the honey, wholegrain mustard and parsley in a large bowl and mix well, seasoning with a little freshly ground black pepper. Add the hot sausages to the bowl and toss them to coat them in the glaze.

Serve the coated sausages in a bowl and give everyone cocktail sticks or small forks to prevent sticky fingers. They are delicious accompanied with sticks of carrot, red pepper and celery.

Tasty, buttery corn on the cob

serves 4 | prep 5 minutes | cook 12 minutes

4 cobs fresh **sweetcorn**

50 g/1¾ oz **unsalted butter**, slightly softened

1 teaspoon **paprika**

1 tablespoon finely chopped **flat-leaf parsley**

Cut each cob in half. Bring a large saucepan of lightly salted water to the boil and blanch the cobs for 5 minutes. Remove them from the pan.

Cook the blanched cobs on a wire rack over the hot coals for 6–7 minutes until they are lightly charred and tender.

Meanwhile place the butter in a small mixing bowl with the paprika and parsley and mix well. Place the cobs on serving plates and divide 'knobs' of the flavoured butter between them, allowing the butter to melt all over. Serve immediately.

Crunchy veggie kebabs

serves **4** | prep **10** minutes | cook **5–6** minutes

1 **courgette**, halved lengthways and cut into chunks

1 small **orange pepper**, deseeded and cut into chunks

1 small **red pepper**, deseeded and cut into chunks

8 **chestnut mushrooms**, halved

2 tablespoons **olive oil**

For the glaze

1 tablespoon **tomato ketchup** or **Clever Tomato Sauce** (see page 32)

1 tablespoon **clear honey**

1 teaspoon **Dijon mustard**

Divide the prepared vegetables evenly between 8 well-soaked bamboo skewers or 8 metal skewers, threading them on in a repeating pattern. Lightly brush each kebab with the oil.

Cook the kebabs on a wire rack over the hot coals for 5–6 minutes, turning occasionally, until the vegetables are lightly charred in places and tender.

Meanwhile make the glaze. Mix together the tomato ketchup or Clever Tomato Sauce, honey and mustard.

Remove the kebabs from the heat and lightly brush them with the glaze.

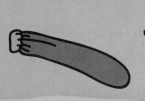

Banana chocolate treasure

serves **4** | prep **10** minutes | cook **10-12** minutes

4 ripe **bananas**

4 tablespoons **golden syrup**

100 g/3½ oz **plain chocolate**, roughly chopped

½ teaspoon **cinnamon**

Vanilla ice cream, to serve (optional)

Slit each banana in half along its length. Place each banana half on a piece of aluminium foil large enough to wrap it up.

Before you wrap, drizzle each length of banana with ½ tablespoon of the golden syrup, then scatter each with a little of the chopped chocolate. Finish with a sprinkle of the cinnamon.

Wrap the banana lengths, scrunching up the foil and leaving a small air pocket at the top of each parcel to let out the steam.

Place the foil-wrapped bananas on a wire rack over the hot coals and cook for 10–12 minutes until the bananas are soft and the sauce is hot.

Serve with a spoonful of vanilla ice cream (if using).

Fruity mallow kebabs

serves **4** — prep **10** minutes — cook **1** minute

1 slightly underripe **banana**, cut into chunks

8 **strawberries**, hulled

½ firm **mango**, stoned and cut into chunks

8 **marshmallows**

½ teaspoon **cinnamon**

Divide the fruit and marshmallows between 4 soaked bamboo skewers or 4 metal skewers.

Place the kebabs on a wire rack over the hot coals and cook for 20–30 seconds on each side until the marshmallows start to go soft and gooey (don't leave them too long or they will melt completely).

Sprinkle the cinnamon over the kebabs and serve immediately, while the marshmallows are still soft.

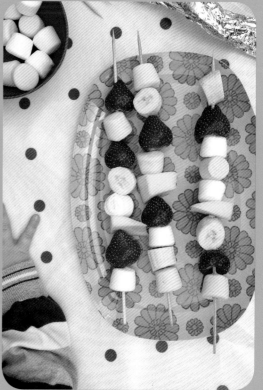

Index

Thank you

A big thank you to all of the Ella's Kitchen employees and friends who contributed recipes for this book and 'road-tested' them with their own families.

A special thank you to all our little helpers – and their parents and carers – for their patience in front of the camera. Here's a list of our little stars and their ages on the days of our photo shoots:

Adam Bennett (age 3)
Alexander Rogoff (age 3)
Amélie Fricker (age 4)
Amélie Holladay (age 3)
Anna Thomas (age 3)
Annabelle Wilson (age 5)
Ava Di Palma (age 2)
Bella Douglas (age 2)
Ben Fleming (age 2)
Bruce Feng (age 5)
Callum McDonnell (age 1)
Carys Davies (age 3)
Charlie Douglas (age 4)

Charlie Newman (age 18 months)
Chloe Dale (age 3)
Conor Rennard (age 2)
Daisy Hawke (age 2)
Dan Heskia (age 5)
Daniel Woods (age 2)
Dhruv Reddi (age 2)
Dylan Standen (age 2)
Elodie Ramus (age 18 months)
Emily Preddy (age 3)
Emma Clements (age 3)
Ethan Wilson (age 7)
Finley Mason (19 months)
Florence Partridge (20 months)
George Hawke (age 4)
Harrison Slaughter (age 2)
Jackson Brooks-Dutton (age 2)
Jessica Brahams (age 3)
Keeley Carson (age 2)
Marnie Clew (age 2)
Michaela Bruce (age 4)
Millie Roxburgh (age 4)
Noah Quinn (age 3)
Olivia O'Brien (age 4)
Olivia Thaw (age 3)

Ollie Woodall (age 3)
Otis Lindsay (age 3)
Parisa A Sadique (age 2)
Poppy Kelly (age 1)
Poppy Nightingale (age 2)
Rosie Beverley (age 2)
Sam Hullis (age 4)
Sebastian Chippindale-Vives (age 2)
Sofia Walker (age 2)
Theo Hendry (age 2)
Tom Crickmay Rack (age 2)
Tyler Thaw (age 4)
Xanthe Grayburn (age 2)

For letting us take photos at their homes, for providing recipe inspiration and all of the other important stuff that was needed to make our very first cook book:

Vanessa Bird, Michelle Bowen, Lee Faber, Nicki Harrold, Catherine Hullis, Alison Lindley, Anita Mangan, Mikha Mekler, Jane Middleton, Victoria Millar

Stickers!

Stars and hearts for the recipes you love
and more to decorate your pages!

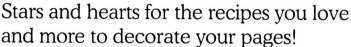

yummy!

I cooked this!

smells good!

crunch!

squishy

scrummy

my favourite

mmmmm!

I cooked this for
_____

I cooked this for
_____

I cooked this for
_____

high 5!

high 5!

high 5!

high 5!